CW00520613

IN A
PRYOR LIFE

The parallel and contrasting lives of
legendary Richard Pryor and his son.

RICHARD PRYOR JR.
WITH RON BRAWER

Copyright © 2019 Ron Brawer and Richard Pryor Jr.

In a Pryor Life
Richard Pryor Jr. and Ron Brawer
Copyright © 2019 Ron Brawer and Richard Pryor Jr.
No part of this book may be reproduced in any form or by any means, electronic, mechanical, digital, photocopying, or recording, except for inclusion of a review, without permission in writing from the publisher or Author.

Published in the USA by:
BearManor Media
P O Box 71426
Albany, Georgia 31708
www.bearmanormedia.com

ISBN: 978-1-62933-388-5
BearManor Media, Albany, Georgia
Printed in the United States of America
Text design by Robbie Adkins, www.adkinsconsult.com
Cover design by Bernie Furshpan, www.Furshpan.com

I dedicate this book to my mom, Patricia Price, for without you I would not be here. Mom, you were my rock and my heart. You instilled in me all the beauty life offers.

BACKSTORY

Mom (Patricia Beatrice Watts) and Dad (Richard Pryor) met in Peoria, Illinois in 1960. She was 16, he was 20. They fell in love and got married.

My mother was a woman who spoke her mind, often with a sharp tongue; my father had a hair-trigger temper.

The newlyweds lived in a house owned by Dad's grandmother—Grandma Marie—who also owned a pair of Peoria whorehouses.

One evening as Mom prepared dinner Grandma Marie noticed a bruise on her face.

"Pat," she said, "what's that? And don't tell me you bumped into a door."

My mother looked away, sheepish and embarrassed.

Marie pressed on: "Richie? He hit you?"

Mom hesitated, shrugged, then nodded her head.

"Why?"

"I made baked potatoes."

"He hit you on account you made baked potatoes?"

"He's sick of potatoes. I cook them a lot. They're cheap and there's different ways to make 'em. Sometimes he gets so mad he throws his plate against the wall."

"And hits you."

"Sometimes."

"Okay, Child, listen. Grab that skillet there."

Mom reached for a skillet hanging on the wall.

"No, the big cast iron one."

Mom took the big cast iron one.

"It's kinda heavy, Mama."

"That's the idea. Now raise it up and bring it down."

Mom did.

"Not like you're shooing away a mosquito. Bring it down *hard*, like you *mean* it."

Mom swung that thing like a sledge hammer.

"Yeah. Now, set it on the stove in easy reach. And next time Rich-ie raises a hand to you, you grab it and *wap* him upside the head."

Mom set the skillet on the stovetop.

Grandma Marie sat down, lit up a Pall Mall cigarette, took a puff, and asked, all innocent, "So, Pat, what's for dinner?"

Mom let a smile play across her face. "Fried chicken. And I could whip up some mashed potatoes and gravy."

"I would *love* me some mashed potatoes and gravy."

When Dad arrived for dinner and sat down at the table Grandma Marie turned her chair sideways for a better view of the proceedings.

Mom set out three plates of fried chicken with, yeah, the mashed potatoes and gravy.

Sure enough, Dad glanced at his plate, grabbed it and heaved it against a wall. Then he stood up and slapped Mom: a back-handed swipe that sent her reeling.

She grabbed the cast iron skillet by the handle and raised it up.

For a split-second Dad stared dumbfounded at that thing, and then *wap!* she brought it down on his head, *hard*. Knocked him cold.

He fell to the floor and landed across Grandma Marie's feet.

She daintily slid her feet out of the way, repositioned her chair, and started eating.

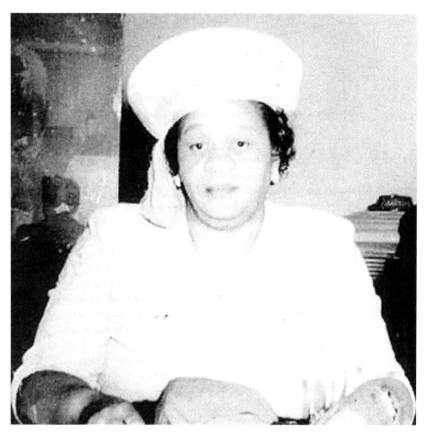

Grandma Marie, late 1940s.

Mom's Side

My mother was born in St. Louis but raised in a town called Louisiana, Missouri.

It's one of those small all-American towns where everybody knows everybody and knows their business. I went there one time to look up an aunt of mine. I went to the house where she once lived, many years ago, and knocked on the door.

An elderly Black woman opened the door.

I said, "Sorry to bother you, ma'am, but my Aunt Verelee used to live here. Do you know where she is now?"

"Oh, Verelee, sure, she moved about a mile away. Here, I'll give you the address."

Granny.

When my mother was growing up the town of Louisiana, like much of Missouri, was subject to Jim Crow laws. When she and her friends went to the movies they had to sit in the "Colored's" section. If they needed to use the restroom they weren't allowed to use the theater's "Whites Only" one, they had to walk down the block to a gas station.

Mom's parents were Gladstone Watts, who everybody called Fox, and his wife, Jessie Davis Watts, who we all called Granny.

They moved from Missouri to Peoria for better employment opportunities. Grandpa Fox got a well-paying janitorial job at St. Francis Hospital. He was old-school: hard-working, responsible, and, aside from this one time he shot and killed a guy in a bar, a do-the-right-thing gentleman.

Granny was a meticulous housewife with an ever-present Viceroy cigarette in hand. She was also a confirmed hypochondriac, at various times convinced she had contracted this or that fatal disease and was soon to die from it.

Even before Grandpa Fox learned of the skillet incident, it was clear to him that my parents were like fire and gasoline. One time he took Dad aside and told him, "Richard, look, if you ever get tired of being married, please just bring her back."

My father did get tired of being married and did bring her back. And each time she ran right back to Dad.

Hey, she was 17, a teenager in love.

DIGRESSION

Okay, I know you want to hear about Grandpa Fox killing that guy in a bar, so let's flash-forward a few years to when I was four.

After work and on weekends Grandpa liked a nip or two of scotch.

One evening in the Globe Street Tap, a bar across the street from Fox and Granny's apartment, he got into a dispute with another patron: The Downstate Illinois Rivalry, a/k/a The Route 66 Rivalry, one of the fiercest contentions in sports.

On one side, the north side, are die-hard Chicago Cubs fans.

Grandpa Fox.

Opposing them are those southern Illini whose proximity to Missouri makes them St. Louis Cardinals rooters.

Grandpa Fox, from Missouri, was firmly in the Cards camp.

The bar argument got heated. Finally, the Cubs fan unloaded what he figured was the clincher: he unzipped his fly, pulled out his penis, thrust it in Grandpa's face, and told Fox to *suck my dick!*

Grandpa calmly knocked back the last drop of scotch in his shot glass, got up off the bar stool, and stormed out.

He crossed Globe Street, entered the two-family house where he and Granny lived, walked up the stairs to their second-floor apartment, and tip-toed in.

Four-year-old-me sat in the living room at a table with a new box of Crayola crayons and coloring book. I looked up when Fox came in. "Hi, Grandpa."

He put a finger to his lips: *shhhh.*

Granny was talking on the phone and puffing away at a Viceroy cigarette, her back to us.

Fox silently entered the bedroom.

Curious about the *shhhh,* I stood and followed him.

He went straight to the chest of drawers, yanked open a drawer, pushed some socks and underwear aside, and took out a pistol.

I ran back into the living room. "*Granny!*"

"Not now, Richie, I'm on the phone."

"But *Granny!* Grandpa—"

"—*Richard!* It's *long distance!*"

Gun in hand, Fox tore out of the apartment.

"*Granny!*"

"*Not now!*"

I went to the window and watched Grandpa cross Globe Street and enter the bar.

A minute later, I heard the shot, *BAM!*

Fox copped a guilty plea in exchange for a reduced sentence: Two years in prison, due to the fact that he had been provoked and had no prior record.

And also, probably, because the guy he killed wasn't White.

DAD'S SIDE

My father's birth mother was a prostitute in one of Grandma Marie's whorehouses. She ran off when Dad was ten, leaving him to be raised by Grandma Marie in one of her brothels.

My father's father, Leroy Buck Carter Pryor—Grandpa Buck—a former boxer, was the brothel enforcer should any of the customers get rowdy or any of the girls need a whupping.

Given that environment, it's no surprise that Dad was physically and sexually abused.

He never talked to me about it, but he certainly continued to rain down physical abuse onto his numerous wives and girlfriends.

And children.

Grandpa Buck.

Arrival!

I entered this world on April 10, 1962, in St. Francis Hospital, Peoria, Illinois, at 2:51 a.m.

I weighed 2 pounds 3 ounces.

Had I been a brook trout or a striped bass, I would've been tossed back.

Instead, the doctor held me up and said, "Congratulations, Mrs. Pryor, it's a boy!"

Then he took a closer look and said, "No, wait, it's a girl."

Then he put his glasses on and looked again. "No, it *is* a boy."

My mom screamed, "*What did I have? A freak?*"

WHAT'S IN A NAME?

My mother had a cousin in Detroit named Rodney Clay, a name she liked and bestowed on me: Rodney Clay Pryor.

The thing is, Dad had a friend named Rodney Clay, and this Rodney happened to be the Rodney Clay who introduced Mom and Dad. My father, at age 21, even before the drugs and booze worked their magic on him, was already somewhat insecure and paranoid. Fearing that Mom and his friend Rodney were lovers (they weren't) and that I might be Rodney's kid (I'm not), a day after I was born he went to the hospital administration and changed the name on my birth certificate.

~~Rodney Clay Pryor~~ => Richard Pryor Jr.

My mother found out about the switcheroo when she came to the hospital to check on me and was told they had no baby there named Rodney Clay Pryor.

"What?"

"Sorry, ma'am."

"Listen, I'm Patricia Pryor and I gave birth to him right here."

"Oh. Well, we do have a preemie, but his name is Richard Pryor, Jr."

Years later, Dad confided that had he known how famous he would become, he never would have named me after himself.

I think what he meant was the name bore a heavy weight, one I would have to carry through life, perceived as Richard Pryor's son and the inevitable comparison; his success, his fame, his wealth.

Dad also understood that most anyone I would ever met, or be attracted to, or fell in love with, I would never be certain if it was me they loved or if they just wanted to bask in the second-hand aura of my dad.

He also knew what I would discover eventually: that there were mean, ruthless people out there who would try to use and manipulate me to get close to him.

Profound words from the world's most famous comedian.

Dad and Me.

DAD HITS THE ROAD

Two weeks after I was born my weight reached five pounds and the hospital released me.

Meanwhile, my parents were so poor that Dad couldn't even afford a notebook. He used to scribble his jokes down on the paper liners from wire coat hangers Grandpa Fox got from the dry cleaner.

Fox bugged Dad nonstop to get a job. One time he sat him down and made him fill out an employment application for St. Francis Hospital, where Grandpa worked.

Dad listed his job experience as "bartender." That was because he spent a lot of time in bars and clubs, where he could perform five minutes of comedy or sing with the band in exchange for drinks and a few dollars.

(One night, at Harold's Club, my mother was there in the audience. Dad sang a love song to her. She was in heaven, delighted that he made her feel so special. Then she happened to glance over her shoulder and realized that Dad was actually singing to a White lady seated right behind her. Dad's earnings for the night went to pay for the shattered bottles and glasses.)

The evening after Dad was to show up for his job interview, Fox asked him, "Did you go to the hospital?"

"Yeah, but they were closed."

It never occurred to him that a hospital was like a police station or fire department, not a grocery store.

Dad's own father, Grandpa Buck, became so frustrated with Dad's lackadaisical attitude toward employment that he kicked us out of Grandma Marie's house. We moved in with Grandpa Fox and Granny, which was why I was there four years later, when Fox got the gun and shot the guy in the bar.

After Dad became rich and famous Mom's sister, Aunt Angie, noted how sad and ironic it was that he took care of his own parents, who kicked him out, but totally ignored and neglected her and Mom's parents, Fox and Granny, who took him in.

When I was four months old Dad "borrowed" a typewriter from his half-sister, Aunt Barbara. He sold the typewriter, bought a bus ticket to New York, and told my mother he'd be gone for three months to pursue his dream of becoming a comic.

When he did return to Peoria he marveled that I could walk already.

"*Of course* he can walk," Mom said, "he's *three years old!*"

Cheers!

I was three the first time I got drunk.

It was on a nice warm day in the park. I was out with Mom and her friends, who were sharing gossip, laughing, drinking, and having a good time.

Somebody must have thought it would be funny to give the kid a sip of booze. Or maybe I was acting up, annoying them, and someone suggested a nip or two would settle the brat down, maybe put him to sleep.

Whatever the reason, they fed me a shot.

I staggered around, dizzy, and fell down. Stood up, staggered around, fell down.

Grandpa Fox came along and gave them hell.

We got into somebody's car and drove through the park. I puked my guts out all over the back seat.

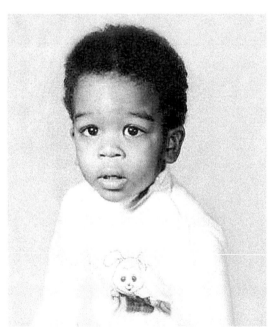

Me, in a sober moment.

RICHARD WATKINS

1964.

Two years after Dad left Peoria Mom concluded that Dad wasn't returning to the fold.

She started dating.

She met Richard Watkins and they moved in together. A year later, she gave birth to my half-sister, Tammi, in St. Francis Hospital, the same hospital I was born in. Since Mom was still legally married to Dad, Tammi's birth certificate reads "Tamela Pryor," not "Tamela Watkins."

Fatherhood did not agree with Richard Watkins. His parents lived in St. Paul, Minnesota. Soon after Tammi was born he deserted us and split for St. Paul.

Harry

Mom moved on.

Through her brother she met Harry Price and took up with him.

It was understandable. Harry came across as a kind and decent guy. He worked for Ozark Airlines as a ground crew maintenance man, cleaning the insides of airplanes—a good, respectable, well-paying job. Plus, there was a fringe benefit: every evening he'd bring home a bag of those little bottles of booze the airline served on flights.

Harry prided himself on being a good provider, always making sure there was food on the table and that Mom wouldn't have to worry about paying the bills.

Truly, he was a kind and decent gentleman.

Except after a few drinks. Which was every night after work and all day Saturday and Sunday.

On those occasions, he had a tendency to beat the shit out of my mother.

I was too young to know what was going on. All I knew was one fine day Mom packed up Tammi and me and we boarded the train to St. Paul.

Harry Price.

THE LAND OF SKY-BLUE WATER

Watkins was happy to reunite, but his parents were another story. For whatever reason, they refused to accept Tammi as their grand-child, and showed even less love for Mom and me.

And Watkins became as abusive as Harry.

(It breaks my heart to report this, but every man my mother was ever involved with was abusive. Not one guy ever treated her like the wonderful woman she was.)

Two months in St. Paul and Mom was done with him.

(When I was twelve, the news trickled down from St. Paul: Rich-ard Watkins had tried to break up a knife fight between two wom-en, one of whom alleged to be his new girlfriend, the other alleged to be his former girlfriend. The details were hazy, but bottom line, Richard Watkins was stabbed to death.)

THE TROUBLE WITH HARRY

Harry heard that we'd returned to Peoria.

He swore to Mom that he had worked out all his anger, and if they got back together he would be the kindest, most decent man ever.

They got back together.

As the saying goes, "It was the triumph of hope over experience."

A lot of the trouble was alcohol-fueled. Harry had those little bottles of airline booze he brought home every night, and Mom liked her beer. After a few brews she might mention this or that flaw in Harry's character, and he would respond aggressively.

One time they lay in bed joking around, laughing like kids. She gave him a playful little shove, and he shoved right back, a tad less playful. Another push, another shove, back and forth, escalating, until she shoved him right off the bed.

That was it.

Fists.

Sobs.

Blood.

Bruises.

Mom always forgave him.

When I was in second grade they got married, which surprised me because I'd always assumed they already were.

Two years later, when I was 10, my half-sister Elanda was born.

Among his other charms, Harry was a womanizer. One night he didn't bother to come home at all. When he did arrive, Mom confronted him.

"Where were you!?"

"Don't ask me questions. I do what I wanna do."

"We're *married*! You can't be carrying on like that."

At which point he grabbed her head and hit it against the wall.

Mom suffered from migraines.

I tried to intercede, he tossed me aside.

I ran for the phone to call the police, he grabbed the phone from my hands and ripped the cord from the wall.

Then he resumed pounding my mother.

WIFE #2

Meanwhile, in New York City. . . .

Dad worked his way up from performing at dinky little Greenwich Village comedy clubs to top of the heap: guest appearances on network television.

Dad on the The Ed Sullivan Show. *Photo Credit: Watkins.*

He also had a steamy affair with, among others—among many others—Maxeine Silverman. They had a baby, my half-sister Elizabeth.

Then he hooked up with Shelley Bonus and wanted to marry her.

One obstacle: he was still legally married to Mom, and Illinois was a fault divorce state. So he filed for divorce based on a claim of adultery, which was ludicrous given his history of fuckery.

How he could prove adultery was through his cousin, a nurse in St. Francis Hospital, where Tammi was born. The cousin snuck into the records room, illegally swiped Tammi's birth certificate, and gave it to Dad. Since Dad could prove he hadn't been with Mom in years, Tammi couldn't possibly be his child, therefore Mom

Dad on The Tonight Show.
Photo Credit: unknown.

Dad with Shelley.

must have had sex with another man, therefore adultery, therefore divorce decree.

Dad married Shelley.

He brought her to Peoria to meet Grandma Marie.

Grandma liked Shelley right away. Shelley was sweet and intelligent. Maybe a little cuckoo-for-cocoa-puffs, some might say, but real sweet and intelligent.

Dad bought me a pair cowboy boots just like his, and roller skates. Shelley, an expert skater, very kindly tried to teach me how to skate. Unfortunately, I fell backward and smacked into her.

(Sorry, Shelley!)

Pretty soon, Dad and Shelley had a daughter, my half-sister Rain, who I met in Los Angeles when I was 11. We're still close.

COBBLESTONE STREETS

I grew up on the south side of Peoria in a predominantly African-American neighborhood. There was a grocery store, a big old Baptist church, a dry cleaner, shoe repair place, pharmacy, every kind of shop you might need. We didn't have to go anywhere because everything was right in our 'hood.

The streets were paved with cobblestones. When a car drove down the block its tires made a sound like wind blowing. In my mind, I can still hear that sound.

Mom was into housewife chores—cooking, ironing, laundry, the whole nine yards. The family called her Donna Reed. (Google it.)

For fun, she liked to hang out with her friends and family, in bars, in the park, at cookouts, at drive-in movies. Her favorite movie was *Gone with the Wind*.

Musically, it was the James Brown era. My mother also loved Jackie Ross, a female soul singer.

Mom worked at a nursing home. She was placed in charge of cleaning dentures. She was supposed to label each set of dentures with the owner's name, but the dentures freaked her out—they were smelly, yucky, and spooky. So instead of labeling them she just tossed them all into a basin with the sterilizer solution. That ended her denture-cleaning job.

Before I started pre-K I spent most of my days with Granny. She'd take me to the playground, maybe buy me a coloring book. With Grandpa Fox away in prison, she had plenty of time for me.

WHOREHOUSE LIFE

Less often, I hung out at one of Grandma Marie's brothels.

It was a three-story building with four bedrooms and two bathrooms on the second floor and third floor. Each bedroom had a large bed, a wash basin on a nightstand, and towels and linens. All the bedrooms were perfumed, smelling of lilacs and roses.

The ground floor had a bathroom, a large living room/reception area with a long couch that Grandma Marie always called a davenport. The walls were done in red textured wallpaper.

There was also a kitchen that had a long counter with a breadbox; inside the breadbox, a loaded gun was always kept.

The system was: a gentleman would knock on the front door and be greeted by Grandma Marie, Grandpa Buck, or his beautiful wife, Grandma Ann. They'd ask the client what service he wanted—or maybe the gentleman had a regular girl—and hook him up.

A lot of politicians patronized the house, which meant Grandma never got busted.

Even as a teen in junior high school I sometimes dropped by and played gin with one or another of the girls to while away the time between their tricks. Periodically, my gin partner would toss down her cards, get up from the table and say, "Hang on a minute, Richie, I gotta go fuck."

MOM'S DREAM

My mother's dream, never realized, was to become a mortician. Why a mortician?

"Dead people," she'd say, "are the only ones who'll never hurt you."

Later in life, when Dad was rich, he offered to send her to mortician school.

She said, "Hell, I'm old enough to be in the casket myself now."

TAMMI

My half-sister Tammi, three years younger than me, was so light-skinned we called her the Pink Panther.

She had fainting spells. They could happen any time, any place: *whoops* and down she'd go.

Once, helping Mom with the laundry, she almost strangled herself, her necklace somehow got caught in the electric wringer.

Luckily Mom shut the wringer just in time, grabbed a scissors, and cut the necklace.

Like our mother, Tammi had a mouth on her and spoke her mind. Even in kindergarten kids wanted to beat her up.

Defending her at a baseball game in the park, I got my arm broken.

Tammi said something to this girl and the girl went at her with a bat. I stuck out my arm to protect my little sister, and *crack!* Broken arm.

When I was in the third grade Tammi started kindergarten at the same school I was in, the Franklin School on Columbia Terrace.

On a typical school day Mom woke us up early in the morning, while it was still dark, and hustled us sleepy-eyed across the street, still in our pajamas, to my cousin and godmother Karen's. Mom and Harry went to work, Tammi and I went back to sleep until Karen woke us up again and got us ready for school.

Kindergarten for Tammi was a half day; she'd be dismissed at the same time my lunch hour started. I'd be on line in the cafeteria, get my lunch, sit down at a table, and there she'd be, ready to leave. I'd wolf down a bite of lunch, then walk her back to Karen's and *race* back to school for my next class.

I did that all the time.

All the time.

I never had a chance to finish lunch.

Me and the Pink Panther.

EATING MY LIVER

Although at birth I was severely premature and stayed in the hospital until my weight reached five pounds, as a child I had no special diet. I ate everything everyone else ate.

Except for liver.

Whenever my mother made liver, Tammi and I would try to hide it under our potatoes and pretend we'd eaten it.

Mom would threaten us: "You're going to sit there until you eat your dinner!"

Sometimes we'd be at the table for hours because Mom was stubborn and we were just as stubborn. We'd sit there forever.

Back then, there was no such thing as "I'm on a gluten-free diet" or "I have a peanut allergy" or "I'm lactose intolerant."

No. It was eat what's on your plate.

Finally, after years of struggle, Mom gave up. Thereafter, whenever she cooked liver she would also make us hot dogs.

GROWING UP

Yeah, Dad went to New York for three months that became three years; Mom and Harry worked; and I spent a lot of time at Granny's apartment or, sometimes, at Grandma Marie's whorehouse. That's where I learned inappropriate language.

Some of my first words were *pussy, dick,* and *motherfucker,* which I pronounced "mudder-pucker," and which I continued to mispronounce long after I knew it was wrong, because it always got a laugh from the grown-ups.

Another laugh line: Grandma Marie had a son named Richard, so after him and my dad, I used to tell everybody that I was "Richard the turd."

That Richard—Uncle Dicky—was huge. Really tall and easily 400 pounds. He worked for Grandma Marie and took over the brothels after she retired.

Dicky lived in a nice house. Several of the girls stayed there, especially those from out of town. With names like Cinnamon and Frosty and Faye, they'd stay in Peoria for a month or two, make some money, and move on.

On a typical day they'd wake up early afternoon, have their coffee and breakfast, shower, dress, and drive over to the whorehouse to open for business.

When Uncle Dicky was home he'd lie on his bed on his stomach—buck-naked, not a stitch of clothing on—and watch TV and smoke joints.

His wife, Aunt Betty, pretty much ran the business.

And Uncle Dicky, big and hefty as he was, always had a woman on the side.

Grandma Marie also had a daughter, Aunt Maxine. Besides prostitution, Maxine was a bootlegger.

(True fact: At one time, Peoria was the bootleg capitol of the world. Al Capone called it home.)

There's a photo of Maxine in a group of people, some occasion or other, friends crowded together, arms on shoulders, smiling for the camera. Maxine is in the front row with her skirt pulled up, her panties pulled down, and her pussy on full display.

Aunt Maxine had a house in Peoria and another house in Bloomington, Illinois, about 40 miles away.

Typically, when I was four or five years old, I'd be making mud pies in her front yard, a car would pull up and a gent would get out.

I'd ask, "What do you need?"

"Where's Maxine?"

"She's turning a trick. What do you need?"

"Two bottles of hooch."

"Coming up."

And then I'd sell him some bootleg.

All in all, I had a normal, healthy, happy childhood. Right?

Okay, yes, I went through a lot of shit and saw a lot of nastiness—alcoholism, prostitution, abuse, murder—that many people might not have been able to handle. But like they say, whatever doesn't destroy you, makes you stronger.

Agreed?

A DEATH IN THE FAMILY

Grandpa Buck's wife, Grandma Ann, began her professional career as a prostitute in one of Grandma Marie's brothels, but worked her way up to madame. She had been a ravishing, beautiful woman. I've seen photos of her, a knockout.

Then she got cancer, oral cancer, and passed quickly.

Dad came to town for his step-mother's funeral.

Dad in Peoria for Grandma Ann's funeral. Seated: Grandpa Buck and Aunt Maxine. Standing, left to right: Aunt Barbara, Cousin Denise, Shelley, Thomas Bryant, and Dad.

I was six years old and had no idea that my father was already somewhat famous, but I could tell he was important because of how the family behaved. Grandma Marie and Uncle Dicky were in a frenzy with the arrangements: limos for those without cars to shuttle mourners from the funeral parlor to the cemetery to Grandma Marie's house; plenty of food and booze post-funeral; and that all would run smooth for my father's stay in Peoria.

It was a sumptuous event, the whole family was there: Grandpa Buck, Uncle Dicky, Aunt Betty, lots of aunts, uncles, and cousins, and a whole slew of Grandma Marie's prostitutes.

The day of the funeral was bitter cold, a real winter-in-Illinois freeze-a-thon. At the cemetery, as we stood around the coffin shivering, the pastor droned on and on.

Finally, Grandpa Buck commented, "If this takes any longer the bitch can just bury herself." Everyone in earshot cracked up laughing. (Dad actually used that line in a routine and made it even funnier.)

Mom told me we were going to Grandma Marie's house after the funeral and that my father would be there. For the occasion she dressed me in a new blue suit—my first suit ever— purchased with a baby-blue dress shirt and a striped clip-on tie.

At Marie's, the buffet table was crammed with food: fried chicken, baked ham, collard greens, mac-and-cheese, candied yams, and every dessert imaginable.

Mom coaxed me to go over and talk to Dad. I was too shy. Instead, I clung to Grandma Marie's apron.

Marie released my hand. "Go on to your daddy."

I walked over.

"Hi," I said, not yet able to add "Dad" or "Daddy."

He reached into his pocket and handed me a shiny coin, a brand-new silver dollar.

I smiled. "Thank you."

Then he lifted me up for a big hug.

Later, for my afternoon nap, Grandma Marie put me in her bedroom, in her enormous fluffy bed, topped with lilac-scented pillows.

Moments after she tucked me in, kissed me good-night, and went out and shut the door, a relative entered the room. Let's call him Uncle Fingers.

Uncle Fingers had maybe nursed his post-funeral grief with a few too many shots of J&B and also needed a restorative nap.

He got undressed and lay down alongside me. Then he took the opportunity to run his hands and fingers over me, including my private parts.

I lay there frozen, deeply embarrassed and ashamed, but too scared to say anything.

At some point, Grandma Marie opened the door, saw what was going on, and coughed.

Uncle Fingers stopped his exploration, Grandma Marie closed the door and left.

That's all I'm going to say about that.

Really.

Playdates and Pageants and Rape, Oh My!

Every weekend, when I was seven, eight, and nine years old, my mother and her brothers and sisters would get together in one of their basements to chill out from the week, play cards, gossip, listen to music, and drink.

My uncles and aunts all had kids, lots of kids: growing up, my cousins were my playmates.

During the week some of the grown-ups would hit up a Goodwill shop or a Salvation Army and buy Miss America-type costumes for the girls.

On the weekends we staged pageants.

The girls would wear the costumes when they paraded down the basement "runway" strutting their stuff.

For the talent portion of the pageant, the girls performed their specialty: maybe sing a song, tell a story or poem, or do magic tricks.

After the pageant elements were completed, everybody would vote to select the girl who would be crowned Miss Peoria.

We made actual tickets, which we sold to the grown-ups, tickets with dotted lines so when a "customer" was admitted to our theater, their ticket stub was torn in half along the dotted line.

Often, after a funeral, we kids re-enacted the ceremony. First we chose up to see who got to play the deceased. In all modesty, I was a terrific corpse.

We also put on plays. I wrote a play we staged called *The Church of the Children.* That was in Aunt Loretta's basement, which was the largest basement in the family. We moved furniture around to create a set that was like inside a church.

I don't exactly remember the play's story line or any of the dialogue, but I do remember one of my girl cousins was dressed like

Tammi struts her stuff.

this old lady from our church who would rant and rave, raise one hand, and sway back and forth. My cousin imitated her perfectly.

Another play I wrote that we did was *Cindy*, the tale of a Black Cinderella.

A third play—I think it was simply called *The Poor Family*—was about a happy family who happened to be very poor.

On warm days my cousins and I played outside: Red Light Green Light, Ring-a-Levio, Tag, or Dynamite Blue.

Every year we gathered around a TV set to watch the *Wizard of Oz* broadcast.

*Tammi and
Tara—always
Dorothy.*

Afterward we'd stage our own version. It was great fun, even though I never got to play Dorothy, who was always played by Cousin Tara because she had braids.

I was the Cowardly Lion. All the time.

Toward the end of a typical weekend playdate, my cousins and I would have a serious discussion about who was going to be the one to ask if we could all spend the night together.

I'm sure the adults knew the request was going to come at some point, and I'm sure they'd already decided whether or not there'd be an overnight and, if so, where and with whom.

But some of those sleepover nights, with two of my older male cousins, were nights I was molested.

Actually, "molested" is way too clinical a verb.

One cousin would hold me down on the bed with my head pressed into a pillow to muffle my screams, while the other cousin got on top of me and fucked me up the ass.

Then they switched.

Oh, God, it hurt like hell.

The cousins. That's me with the big head, second row, second from the right.

Why didn't I tell Mom?

Mainly, embarrassment.

Also, fear: fear of those cousins retaliating and, absurd as it sounds, fear that snitching would end play dates. No more pageants and plays.

Cousins, Uncles, and Ants

When I was a kid, if a cousin was a grown-up he or she was called Uncle or Aunt.

One uncle, Bobby Anderson, had a boy my age named Bobby Anderson Junior. We always called him Little Bobby.

(Thank God no one ever called me Little Richard.)

Little Bobby and I went to the same school and were often over at Aunt Karen's, so we spent a lot of time together.

I called him recently. He's married, lives in California, and just got out of prison.

"Bobby, you remember one time we were out playing in Aunt Karen's yard and we sat on top of a red ant colony?"

"Oh God, *yes!* Those fuckers swarmed all over us and we were like *screaming!*"

"And Aunt Karen threw us in the bathtub and doused us with water to wash them off."

We had a good laugh over that.

Then he said, "Richie, remember that big rain storm? We were leaving school and there was this, like, huge puddle of water?"

"No, no memory of that."

"You and and me, we're throwing rocks into this puddle to make a mud splash. And there was another kid, real asshole, took a brick and threw it while I was reaching into the puddle for a rock. Fucker busted my thumb open."

"Wait a minute now, yes, I remember Cousin Denise was there and she grabbed my homework and wrapped your bloody thumb with my homework!"

"Yeah, and took me to the emergency room for stitches. I still have a scar there."

Another cousin of mine, up in Detroit, murdered his ex-wife and her boyfriend.

He went to their house, asked to see his kids, and she wouldn't let him. So he shot her in the head in front of the kids, and then killed the boyfriend.

Yeah.

The Detroit branch of the family was notoriously bad mudder-puckers. We never worried about our safety when we visited them.

Class Clown Pees Pants

At Franklin Elementary School, when I was in the fourth grade, my mother came to a parent-teacher conference and was told, "Richard is a terrific student and would do even better if he wasn't always the class clown."

Uh-huh, the class clown, that be me.

In retrospect, I'm sure my behavior was a result of feeling distanced from my classmates. I turned to clowning as a way to earn approval from my peers, to be part of the group, to belong.

As a result, I became "teacher's worst nightmare," and often had to stay after school in detention.

On one occasion detention must have run later than usual because the janitor had already cleaned the bathrooms and locked the doors.

And I had to pee. Bad.

I tore out of school and ran home. Two blocks from the house I started to dribble in my pants. I quickened my pace, the dribble turned into a flow.

When I arrived home and ran up the front stairs I saw my step-dad, Harry, sitting in the living room.

We were not supposed to use the front door.

I raced around to the back yard, where I hesitated, thinking, *I don't want to go inside and tell them I pissed all up and down the block.*

So I snuck in quietly, tiptoed down to my room in the basement, and slid out of those sopping wet pants.

The house rule was, we always had to wear our clothes two days in a row, and my peed-in pants happened on *Day One*. I would have to wear those pants again tomorrow. I hung them in the closet to dry.

In the morning, Mom pressed the pants. The heat of the iron on that dry urine hit her like a stink-storm.

"*Richard!*" she screamed.

Yeah, I should have warned her.

I got whupped for that.

ABOUT WHUPPINGS

In our house, a whupping was a formalized ritual. The whuppee was ordered out to the back yard to fetch a "switch."

You'd go out to the willow tree, break off a low-hanging branch, and strip the leaves away, leaving a whip-like length of greenery: A switch.

And woe unto you if you returned with a feeble-looking switch. That would only anger the whupper and you'd be hauled back out into the yard where you'd tremble in fear as a sizable willow branch was converted to a Weapon of Ass Destruction.

WORST WHUPPING OF ALL TIME

The worst whupping I ever got was the time I beat Tammi over the head with a Pepsi bottle.

I swear I didn't mean to hurt her.

The thing is, I'd seen a lot of Western movies, how, in a bar fight, characters would smash people over the head with a liquor bottle and the bottle would break.

So I took a Pepsi bottle and hit her over the head with it.

She screamed.

My mother was on the phone, heard the scream, and looked over at us.

I assured my sister, "Hang on, Tammi, it'll break."

And I hit her over the head with the Pepsi bottle again.

In one second flat Mom had a hairbrush in her hand and began to whale on my ass.

I got tore up big time.

Bruises and welts for days.

Sibling Revenge

We had a garden in the back yard with all kinds of fruits and vegetables.

Mom would make preserves, jams, jellies, stewed tomatoes, all that Donna Reed stuff.

The kitchen counter wasn't a hard surface; if you pushed hard you could indent it.

So one time I took a knife and carved it up.

Tammi took the fall.

Another time, I was twelve, Tammi was nine, and our little sister, Elanda, was three.

Tammi and I were playing around with the screen door and it broke.

So we went outside, propped the door back up, and called baby sister out to play with us.

She pushed the screen door and it toppled over.

Yeah, Elanda did it.

Fox

Before Grandpa Fox shot and killed the guy in the bar he was a functioning alcoholic. After he got out of prison, he didn't drink.

He had three favorite TV shows: *Lawrence Welk*, *Hee-Haw*, and *Gunsmoke*. Whenever I was there watching TV with him I'd lie across his lap and he'd scratch my back like I was a puppy-dog.

I still love to have my back scratched.

He and Granny slept in separate bedrooms because Granny snored, loud.

One night she was woken up by a thump from Grandpa Fox's bedroom. She went in and there he was, lying on the floor. He'd had a stroke.

She called an ambulance and he was rushed to the hospital but never recovered. He died April 7, 1972. Three days before my tenth birthday.

At the funeral parlor I brought this toy he had given me, a plastic horse with woolen strands for a tail and mane. I put it in his casket.

It was the first time I ever saw a dead body. It looked like he was just asleep. I touched his hand, it was icy cold, so cold it scared me. I stood and stared at him, stared so long that I thought I could see him breathing.

After the funeral the family gathered at Granny's house. Everybody went out of their way to be super nice to me because it was such a sad event right on my birthday. There were gifts, everybody sang the Birthday Song, and there was a birthday cake with ten candles. I don't remember what wish I made before blowing out the candles, but I remember how incredibly close to my family I felt on the day of Grandpa Fox's funeral.

Welcome to LAX!

The summer after Fox died was the first time I spent a solid chunk of time with my father.

I was excited about the flight to California. Mom took me to the airport and handed me over to a stewardess who stuck a pin onto my shirt that said UNACCOMPANIED MINOR.

Dad's house was in Laurel Canyon, up in the Hollywood Hills. The house was a rental and it was on stilts—*a house on stilts!*—which was also a pain, because after you parked your car you had to walk up these long wooden flights of stairs to the house. It was a particular drag if you were carrying groceries or luggage or anything.

The house itself smelled like cat pee.

It was just Dad, me, and his girlfriend, Patricia von Heitman, a pretty German woman.

That summer Dad was booked to host Wolfman Jack's TV show, *Midnight Special.*

A few days before the show we went shopping and Dad bought us matching suits.

I sat in the audience for the taping. At some point in the show Wolfman Jack found me and asked me how old I was.

The correct answer, remember, was *ten.*

"Nineteen," I said.

Which drew a huge laugh. Ah, a chip off the old block.

Dad was always up most of the night and slept through half the day.

At home in Peoria, if I wasn't in school or running errands for Mom I could always play outside in the playground, either alone or with friends. In Laurel Canyon, though, I had no friends and there was no playground.

So, that summer, I had to fend for myself, which meant granola for breakfast—my first encounter with granola—and cartoons on TV.

The next summer, the summer I was 11, Dad's star had risen to where he rented a much nicer house, also in the Hollywood Hills but more accessible. Everything inside was sparkling and new, with no cat pee smell.

And there was a swimming pool.

During the day I could go outside and sit by the pool or practice my basketball skills with a hoop mounted on the garage. But there were no other kids to play with until, one day, we got in the car and Dad told me we were going to a friend's house who had a son about my age.

When we got to the house, we were welcomed by...

Billy Dee Williams!

(Billy Dee Williams, star of *Brian's Song*, *Lady Sings the Blues*, and later, for you *Star Wars* fans, as Lando Calrissian in *The Empire Strikes Back* and *Return of the Jedi*.)

I was so awed, my mouth dropped open and I stood there gaping. Dad gave me a weird look.

Then Billy's son, Corey, popped in. He was about my age, maybe a year or two older. Both of us grew up as the son of a famous father, so we had a lot in common and really hit it off.

On the drive home Dad was sulky.

"How come," he asked, "you never look at *me* like that?"

He meant the way I'd stared at Billy Dee Williams. I guess, in my mind, Dad was just my my father—not a big movie star.

That weekend he had a swimming pool party at the house. It's where I first met my sisters, Rain and Elizabeth.

There were a lot of celebrities lounging around. I can't remember who they were, but I do remember that Dad thought it would be highly entertaining to pick me up and toss me into the pool.

I didn't know how to swim. I was frantic, clawing the water, going under, almost drowning, but somehow I got to the edge of the pool and climbed out.

Dripping wet, I turned to Dad and yelled, in front of everybody, "*You motherfucker!*"

Dad and me at the pool.

UNCLE TOM'S FAIRY TALES

It was great having my sisters to play with. We made movies together. Like, after we saw *The Exorcist* we acted it out. The girls lay on the bed and I got under the bed and kicked the mattress, making them laugh hysterically as they flopped around like Linda Blair.

Dad was in the process of shooting a movie himself, so he had all this professional equipment in the house.

His project started because he was very frustrated at not getting more film work and feeling stuck in a rut, just doing stand-up comedy. Rain's mom, Shelley, urged him to take the money from their wedding gifts and use it to produce his own film.

Uncle Tom's Fairy Tales is about a White guy who raped a Black woman and is on trial facing an all-Black judge and jury, played by Dad's friends.

Between takes they all drank Courvoisier and snorted cocaine.

Dad wrote the script and shot a lot of it, but since the actors were so coked up they kept shooting take after take. Pretty soon the money ran out and everyone involved in the project dropped out. Everyone, that is, besides the film's editor, a woman named Penelope Spheeris.

(Penelope was the only person who stayed with the project after the funding ran out and everyone else quit. The poetic justice here is that she was the only person connected to the project, besides Dad, who went on to have a successful film and TV career.)

When Dad finally had a rough cut of the film, without a music track or color-correction, he arranged a private screening for Bill Cosby. What happened next remains a Hollywood mystery: *Uncle Tom's Fairy Tales* disappeared.

There's been speculation that Cosby, realizing that Dad was his chief competition, bought the film and buried it away.

Another theory: Shelley felt neglected and rejected because Dad was spending every moment working on the film. One night, she went on a cocaine-infused tantrum, screaming that Dad loved his fucking film more than he loved her. Dad responded with his own coke-infused tantrum. To prove he loved her he ripped the film reels from the editing machine and tore them to shreds.

Life with Father

Mom often told me how much she loved me. Dad was rarely that expressive. His way of showing affection was monetary. It wasn't "Let me give you a great big hug!" It was, "Here's some money, Son, buy some clothes."

That second summer with Dad, the summer of the almost-drowning incident when I was eleven, I wound up going to Billy Dee Williams's house a lot. Besides his son, Corey, there was Billy's wife, Teruko, and her daughter, Miyako, who was also our age.

Sometimes we'd hang out in the kitchen, where Teruko taught me how to clean fresh shrimp.

Patricia Von Heitman, Dad's last-year-girlfriend, had been demoted (or *pro*moted, depending on your point of view) to his assistant. Among her other responsibilities, she was tasked with driving Corey and me around town. We'd cruise down Holly-wood Boulevard, and every time we stopped for a red light we'd be mobbed with girls who recognized us and wanted our autographs.

(Eventually, of course, Patricia and Dad had a huge blowout. I don't remember what it was about, probably one of his hook-ups treating Patricia like a servant. Her final words were: "*You can kiss my white German ass!*")

One afternoon Dad dropped Corey and me off at Flip Wilson's house to play with Flip's sons, Kevin, who was around the same age as us, and David, two years older. The dads then went off to do dad stuff, probably snort cocaine and chase pussy.

The four celeb-son kids, alone in the house with no adult super-vision, came across a bowl of marijuana, Flip's stash. Along with the weed, there was a device for separating the stems and seeds, a packet of rolling paper, and a Zippo lighter.

It was David who figured out how to roll a joint.

And that was the first time I got high, eleven years old.

DÓNDE ESTÁ SANTA CLAUS?

On Christmas Morning, Mom, Harry, Tammi, Elanda, and me would open our presents and hang out. In the afternoon, the entire family—aunts, uncles, and cousins—would converge at Granny's. She always made a huge pot of custard and we'd eat custard and compare gifts.

The Christmas I was eleven Granny heard me mention the gifts that Santa left me. She said, "Richie, you know there's no such thing as Santa Claus, right?"

"*What?*"

"You don't believe in Santa Claus any more, do you?"

No Santa Claus? I was in shock, my mind blown.

I looked around the room. All eyes were on me. Even cousins half my age were in on this no-such-thing-as-Santa shit. Apparently, I was the last to know.

"Nah," I said, "Santa Claus is for little kids."

ALONE

At school there were two guys I was friendly with. Otherwise, I didn't feel connected to any of my classmates.

During recess, in the yard, there'd be all these little cliques and groups. The religious kids who went to church a lot would gather together into a mini-choir and sing gospel tunes. Other kids who liked to sing would harmonize on doo-wop tunes. And, of course, the basketball players and baseball players and wrestlers—the jocks—they'd all hang out together.

I felt like a loner.

ART CONTEST

I always loved to draw, even after an event which had a weird effect on me. In the sixth grade my school held an art contest. All the art class students were to submit a Halloween-themed drawing and the principal would pick the winner.

I drew a boy in a ghost costume riding a bicycle down a cobblestone street. While I drew it another boy in class admired the work and told me how good it was.

When I finished, though, I thought it *wasn't* very good and threw it away.

But guess what my admirer did? He drew the exact same picture—a boy in a ghost costume riding a bicycle down a cobblestone street—submitted it, and *won*.

I still think about that, how hurtful it felt. It taught me how people can take things from you and claim them as their own.

It was around then that I started losing interest in art—and school generally. I did everything I could to avoid classes.

I ran for student council and became class treasurer.

Likewise, chorus, drama club, and basketball practice.

Did my grades suffer as a result of missed classes?

Yep.

Speaking of basketball practice, even though I was still physically short, I was on the basketball team. There were two other Black boys on the team, both of them in the starting line-up. And then there was that one Black boy sitting on the bench the entire game, every game.

A Black boy completely inept at basketball: Me.

Ike and Mike

I had two friends in sixth and seventh grade, let's call them Mike and Ike. Mike was a White dude on the basketball team.

Ike was a thief.

His sister and mother were also thieves; they taught me how to shoplift.

We'd go to the IGA or a drug store or hardware store and steal things. Dumb shit like batteries or lip balm or Tic Tacs—stuff we didn't necessarily want or need. It was all about the excitement, the adrenaline high of walking out of a store with a stolen item.

That rush, that high, was a feeling I'd seek to replicate through most of my life.

SEXUAL STIRRINGS

Way before there was eBay and Amazon there were mail-order catalogues like Sears-Roebuck and JC Penney. They were sent out quarterly and Granny always had those catalogues in her house.

Some of my earliest memories are perusing photos in the men's underwear section from those imminently respectable all-American catalogues and studying the bulges in the men's tighty-whities.

I may have glanced at the lingerie sections, but I never dawdled there.

When I hung out with my two junior high school pals, "Mike" and "Ike," we often had overnights at one or another's house. Those overnights were the first times I regularly saw guys my age naked, and the first times I began to feel an attraction for someone who was the same sex as me.

Lionel Runs Away

Out of the blue, my mother started calling me Lionel. It was usually said when I was getting on her nerves for one reason or another.

For example, at dinner, if I was leading Tammi in a liver boycott, she'd say, "Eat your liver, Lionel!"

Or, if there were grown-ups in the house drinking, laughing, and gossiping, that was understood to mean the kids should go play somewhere else. But if I stuck around to hear the gossip, she'd glare at me.

"Get out of here, Lionel!"

It turned out, "Lionel" was a real person. My mother's hairdresser.

When I eventually met him he turned out to be the swishiest queen you could imagine.

I was shocked. Was I really walking and talking and carrying on in such a feminine manner?

And was Mom making fun of me because of my walk?

I was so hurt, that when we got home I started crying.

As I sobbed, I wailed, "Don't nobody loves me, don't nobody care."

I kept repeating it like the chorus of a song: "Don't nobody loves me, don't nobody care." *Sob.* "Don't nobody loves me, don't nobody care." *Sob-sob.* "Don't nobody loves me—"

"—You're right, Lionel! Don't nobody loves you! Don't nobody care!"

With that, I ran away from home.

I got as far as Grandma Marie's station wagon, parked in the street. It was unlocked. I went inside and locked all the doors.

Nobody came to look for me. The longer I sat there, the sadder and more miserable I became. *Don't nobody loves me, don't nobody care.*

Any time someone passed on the street I'd look to see if it was Mom or one of my relatives. No.

Don't nobody loves me, don't nobody care.

The hours passed. It was dinner time and I was hungry. I started to wonder how I'd extricate myself from this situation with dignity intact. Finally, I realized I'd have to swallow my pride.

I returned home.

When I entered the house Mom stood there, hands on hips.

"So you decided to stop sulking," she said.

I shrugged, nodded.

"Okay, go wash your hands for dinner."

After that, Mom stopped calling me Lionel.

And I started to walk with a more manly stride.

What I Want to be When I Grow Up

A garbage man.

Yeah, when I was little that was my dream job. That's all I talked about, being a garbage man. (Freudians, feel free to interpret that.)

After Mom had that class clown conference she clamped down on me. But I think she realized early on that academia was not going to play a big part in my life. Like my father, my talent lay in creativity. She encouraged me in that direction.

When I was seven she started me on piano lessons with Mrs. McCoy, the minister's wife at our church, Zion Baptist.

Pretty soon I could play "Mary Had a Little Lamb." After that I figured, *Okay, now I know how to play the piano, I don't need to take any more piano lessons.*

Today, I can't even play "Mary Had a Little Lamb."

In sixth grade I took up the trombone and was briefly in the school band. The thing was, the constant vibrations from blowing into that trombone made my lips itch.

End of trombone career.

I sang in the church choir and in the school's chorus.

In high school, after a brief obsession with architecture, I got more seriously into acting. Part of it was a sense of family tradition. *Well, Dad is an actor, I could be like that. SHOULD be like that.*

In my freshman year at Peoria Heights I acted in *Any Number Can Die.* For our senior play, it was *Goodnight Ladies.*

Learning lines, attending rehearsals, and remembering blocking took study and work, but the acting part came easy, a natural fit. When you're uncomfortable in your own skin, pretending to be someone else is a relief. It was like God knocking on a door and you open the door and there's everything you ever dreamed of.

As time went on I went through a period where I became jealous of my sister Rain. Dad always boosted her career; she starred

Phyllis Sharp Brecklin and me in Goodnight Ladies.

in TV shows, made films, and created a successful one-woman play for herself.

Me? Sure, I could be a PA (Production Assistant) on his films or read scripts for him to see if they were any good. But every job I had through his influence was behind the camera. Only once, on *Critical Condition*, did he ever say "Why don't you read for this part?"

I think he felt that I, as a man, needed to find my own path in life, while Rain, a girl, deserved all the help she could get.

Jennifer Lee, my father's final wife, once advised me that there was a German saying to the effect that a father doesn't want his son to do the same work as he does because he's afraid that the son will surpass him. She thought that was my father's problem with my acting career.

Advice from Jennifer, though, could be fraught with secret agendas.

The Armando Incident

The summer when I was twelve, Dad's film career was in high gear.

Or maybe it was the summer before. Or maybe a summer or two after. You see, all kinds of fucked-up shit happened to me somewhere between the ages of 12 and 14, and in my mind, all that stuff occurred *when I was twelve.*

So, when I was 12, Dad starred in *The Bingo Long Traveling All-Stars & Motor Kings* with his pal Billy Dee Williams. The film was shot in Macon, Georgia and I was along for the ride.

We stayed in a deluxe hotel, where I had my own room and quickly discovered room service.

Yeah, I became, like, a room service junky. I'd get on the house phone and lower my voice an octave.

"Hello? This is Richard Pryor Junior and I'd like to order a cheeseburger, well-done, an order of French fries, and a Pepsi."

Yum.

Dad had an assistant on the shoot, Armando.

One afternoon Armando asked me to his room to watch TV.

Somehow we ended up on the floor wrestling. Two guys fooling around with tricky wrestling holds. Nothing sexual, right?

Except that something wasn't kosher. Maybe it was the hard object I felt in Armando's crotch every time he bumped up against me, which he kept doing until finally I reached down to see what was going on.

Which was his exact intention, so that if the incident ever came to light he had deniability. He could say I initiated the contact.

I touched his erection and he touched mine.

And then we were both naked and he sucked my cock.

And I sucked his cock.

And he ejaculated all over me.

I was so naïve, my thought was, *Hmmm, this stuff looks like Jurgens lotion.*

Afterward, Armando warned, "Richard, you better not tell anybody about this or you're gonna be in big trouble. Remember, you started it."

The next time I went to his room it was the same thing all over again. The wrestling, the touching, Armando waiting for me to instigate.

Did I enjoy it?

Well, I always enjoy attention and affection, but more than that, I somehow felt like I was *supposed* to do what Armando wanted.

As the summer wore on I started looking forward to the next time, and the next.

You understand, because of where I came from, raised mostly by Grandma Marie in one of her whorehouses and growing up among prostitutes and pimps, I heard in graphic detail about blow-jobs, anal, and dick, so I was mentally quite jaded and never felt what I was doing with Armando was *wrong*.

It's just the way people are.

THE MARY WHITECLOUD INCIDENT

The same summer—or maybe not, maybe it was some other summer *when I was 12*—Dad filmed *Adiós Amigo* with Fred Williamson and James Brown (the former football star, not the Godfather of Soul).

The film was shot in Santa Fe, New Mexico.

This time I shared a room in another five-star hotel with Fred's son, Fred Williamson Jr.—Freddie—who was about my age. Before leaving Los Angeles I'd snagged a baggie of Flip Wilson's weed from Kevin. Freddie and I mostly got high and lounged around the pool or ordered room service.

One day while we watched TV and smoked a joint the house phone rang. It was a call from Mary Whitecloud, an extra on the film.

She said my dad wanted me to come down to her room right away to discuss an important personal matter.

Since only the film's principals (the stars, director, and producers) were housed in this ritzy hotel, while the supporting actors, extras, and production crew were lodged across the street at a Holiday Inn, I probably should have wondered why Mary Whitecloud, a mere extra, had her own room here with the elite.

Right next to Dad's room.

But hey, I was 12 years old and stoned out of my gourd. That kind of logical question didn't occur to me.

So Freddie and I finished the joint and, in swim suits, t-shirts, and flip-flops, traipsed down to Mary's room.

"Freddie," she said, "sorry, but I need to speak with Richard about a very important personal matter."

He shrugged and left.

Mary and I stood there a minute and eyed each other. I'd never paid much attention to her; she was an adult, twenty-five at least. Lots older than me.

That said, I now noticed that Mary Whitecloud was a Native American beauty with silky dark hair that flowed down to her waist, flawless olive-colored skin, and striking hazel-green eyes.

She wore a skimpy little bikini that framed a *Playboy* Bunny body.

She handed me a tube of suntan lotion, from which I figured that the plan was to have our important personal conversation out by the pool.

Instead, she lay down on the bed, on her stomach, and asked me to rub suntan lotion on her back. To help the process she reached behind her and undid her bikini top.

I kicked off my flip-flops, knelt on top of her—knees on either side of her butt—and squirted lotion onto her back.

"Ow. Richard, that's *cold*."

"Sorry."

"First, squeeze some lotion on your hands, then rub them together till the goop is nice and warm, *then* rub it on my back."

I warmed the goop in my hands and massaged her shoulders.

"*Gently.*"

I eased up.

"Much better."

I worked my way from her shoulders to her upper back. Her skin felt smooth and warm to the touch.

"Lower," she said.

I squirted more lotion into my palms, rubbed them together, and massaged her lower back.

She sighed.

I started to get aroused.

"Legs."

I knelt on the floor and started on her left foot. She had a perfect arch.

She kicked her foot away. "That tickles."

"Sorry."

"Do my calves."

I got back on the bed, between her legs, and massaged her calves.

"Higher," she said.

More lotion on trembling hands, a self-conscious hard-on raging in my swim suit.

Her thighs were firm, smooth, luscious.

She moaned, "Mmmm."

Then she reached down and slid out of her bikini bottom—an easy task with all the lotion on her legs.

"Your dad wants me to show you something," she said.

She lifted one leg over my head and down, and rolled onto her back so that I was between her thighs, face-to-face with her neatly-trimmed bush and gorgeous breasts.

She sat up, pulled my t-shirt over my head, and tossed it aside.

She pushed me down onto my back and pulled off my swim suit.

"Nice," she said.

She took the suntan lotion from me, squeezed some onto her hands, and dropped the tube on the floor. She rubbed her hands together, then started to massage my erection.

Oh God, I was about to explode.

"Sit up," she said.

I did. She pulled me down on top of her and guided me inside her.

She ground against me, slowly, in and out.

"Pull out before you come," she said.

Too late.

BIRTHDAY BOY

On my thirteenth birthday Dad was in Chicago and drove down to Peoria with birthday presents.

He showed up with two gifts: a chemistry set and a black velour jogging suit with gold embroidery.

The chemistry set had rows of little glass jars filled with powders; a recipe manual for creating all kinds of mixtures and tinctures and reactions; butterflies, moths, and insects mounted on identification cards; and a dead baby frog preserved in a formaldehyde-filled jar, that you could dissect.

There was also an X-Acto knife for the dissection, a microscope, and several glass slides. After you cut up the frog you could place thin slices on a slide and examine them under the microscope.

Oh boy, I couldn't wait to get my hands on that frog. Seriously. I bounced up and down with happiness and gave Dad a huge hug.

Harry got real offended. Even though he was a hard-working SOB, we were always poor, and he could never afford a gift like that. So he was all riled up about Dad walking into our house like King Shit, when it was *Harry* taking care of me, *Harry* being the Real Father.

He yelled in Dad's face: "You never *been* here for this boy."

And Dad screamed right back at him, "I'm his *dad*, nigga, he come outta *my* dick, not yours."

Harry became even more enraged when he heard the n-word. He hated it and never said it. For Dad, "nigga" was every other word out of his mouth.

Mom managed to calm them down, thank God, because both of them were highly volatile and violence-prone.

Dad swallowed his pride, backed off, hugged me, and exited graciously before an all-out brawl could start.

Two months later, when I graduated from junior high school, Dad, as a graduation gift, invited the entire family—Mom, Harry, Tammi, my baby sister Elanda, and me—on an all-expenses-paid vacation to the Bahamas, including first class airfare and a three-room suite at a deluxe hotel.

Dad had also arranged for Harry, who loved to fish, to spend a day on a Caribbean fishing boat, just him, the captain, and two crew members.

But then Mom, who also loved to fish, found out that the vessel was a glass-bottom boat, where she could not only fish but also observe coral reefs and exotic sea creatures in their natural habitat. At the last minute she decided to join the excursion.

The captain was not pleased about the additional passenger and made a big fuss over it. Mom assured him that he would be paid for the extra passenger.

The captain insisted he had to first speak to my father. He traipsed off and returned a few minutes later, grim-faced.

The two-man crew was equally irked by Mom's presence. She chalked it up to Caribbean machismo.

Nevertheless, she and Harry had a grand time. They observed gorgeous reefs teeming with a myriad of colorful exotic sea creatures. They also landed tarpon, pompano, wahoo, bonefish, and barracuda.

So what was the deal with the captain's reluctance to add my mom?

Years later, I surmised that it was all about the chemistry set Dad gave me, Harry yelling at him in front of Mom and me, and Dad swallowing his pride and exiting graciously.

You see, my father was not the kind of man to swallow his pride and exit graciously. I was 99.9% certain that he had offered the glass-bottom-boat captain and his crew a considerable chunk of change to toss Harry overboard miles out into the Caribbean and leave him there for shark food.

By the way, the day of Mom and Harry's glass-bottom boat trip didn't end well for Tammi and me. We had wanted to spend the day at the beach, but Mom insisted we stay at the hotel pool to keep an eye on baby sister Elanda, who paddled mindlessly around the pool inside a plastic inflatable tube.

But as soon as Mom and Harry left the hotel for their fishing trip, Tammi and I snuck off to the beach. Sure enough, Elanda, in the deep end of the pool, somehow slipped out of the tube and started to drown. The lifeguard jumped in and saved her life.

Later, he reported the incident to Mom.

Yeah, Tammi and I both got a whupping.

Oh, hey, remember that other one of Dad's birthday gifts? The black velour jogging suit with gold embroidery on the jacket? Well, the embroidery spelled EVERY NIGGER IS A STAR.

There was no way I was going to wear that jacket, particularly given Harry's feelings about the n-word. I took a scissors and cut out the offensive word, so all you could see was EVERY   IS A STAR. Whatever I had on underneath filled the space.

I wore that butchered jacket around the house, but never out in public.

THE N WORD

Peoria Heights High School was overwhelmingly White. In the entire school there were only five Black kids.

One day, one of the White boys called me nigger.

I punched him in the face and we fought.

Consequently, we were both suspended for a week.

At home, Harry was very pissed off at me for fighting and the suspension.

But Mom was proud because I stood up to this kid.

Peoria Heights Chorus. Guess which kid is me.

THE TROUBLE WITH HARRY, PART II

Mom and Harry were separated again. He now lived in a mobile home in Kings Park with his current girlfriend.

Over Christmas vacation, Mom went to see him for some reason or other, probably a money matter. As soon as she walked in he said, "Pat, you gotta leave."

"I ain't goin' nowhere," she answered him, then turned to the girl-friend. "We still married, see?"

Harry got threatening: *"You gotta leave NOW!"*

That's when Mom grabbed a kitchen knife and stabbed him in the gut. His girlfriend screamed, grabbed the phone, and called 911.

Harry tried to grab the knife from Mom, but only got his hand cut.

He backed away. Mom came after him. He ducked behind a chair; Mom kicked it aside, closed in, and stabbed him again.

By the time the police arrived Harry had wrestled himself behind Mom and clutched her arms to protect himself, but she still managed to reach back to stab him some more.

Meanwhile, the girlfriend cowered in a corner, trembling.

The police held Mom, handcuffed her, and recited the Miranda. When they got to the part about *You have the right to remain silent*, she screamed, "No, I want to kill the mother fucker."

That Christmas I was in Hawaii with Dad, Deboragh, and my sisters when we got the call. My mother was in jail, charged with attempted homicide.

Dad immediately wired bail money and hired a top criminal defense attorney.

Mom wound up with just probation.

And Dad? I never saw him happier than that Christmas in Hawaii. Every few minutes he burst into laughter for no particular reason. Only, there *was* a particular reason: Harry, the guy who'd insulted him in front of his ex-wife and son, and escaped a Caribbean shark feast, had gotten his come-uppance. And at the very hands of that ex-wife, which was some kind of twisted karma. Delicious. Even more delicious, Harry would now live out the rest of his days with those knife scars on his skin and psyche.

As an extra bonus, the lawyer's fee was probably lots less than what Dad would have had to pay the glass-bottom-boat captain and crew for feeding Harry to the sharks.

If that had, in fact, been Dad's plan.

Dad, happy as a clam, with Deborah, Rain, Elizabeth, and me.

JERK

On another Christmas vacation Dad took Deboragh, Elizabeth, Rain, and me to Jamaica, where we stayed in a villa he rented in Ocho Rios, complete with servants and a cook who prided herself on Jamaican specialties.

We spent a lot of time at our private beach. Dad and Deboragh would sometimes wander down the shore for several minutes. I assumed Dad had found a connection for *ganja*, the local marijuana product. Although I'd smoked weed several times since two summers ago, when Kevin, Corey, and I smoked Flip Wilson's stash, I didn't think it would be a great idea to ask Dad if could get high with him and Deboragh.

No matter. The Caribbean was warm, smooth, and waist-high for a good forty or fifty feet out. Every day the weather was perfect: clear and sunny. While Dad and Deboragh cooled their *ganja*-parched throats with Red Stripe beer, my sisters and I sipped delicious fruit drinks or virgin Piña Coladas that the cook specially prepared for us and were carried out to the beach by a young woman servant whose name we couldn't pronounce but who asked us to call her Doda.

When we weren't at the beach Dad arranged for some private tours. There was Discovery Bay, where Christopher Columbus landed on his way to "discover" America. At the time of his arrival, we learned, the island was populated by the Arawak Indian tribe. Columbus did not bring women on their voyage. Needless to say, when they arrived in Jamaica his crewmen were plenty horny. By force of arms, they readily took Arawak women.

Woe to any Arawak men who fought against the rape of their wives, daughters, or sisters: those men were typically punished by Columbus and his crew by chopping their hands off.

We also visited Rose Hall, a Georgian-style mansion built in the 1770s. It was part of the Palmyra plantation, where, in the Nineteenth Century over 250 African slaves labored. According to legend, the mansion itself was overseen by the notorious "White Witch," who kept a dungeon in the basement where she chained and tortured disobedient slaves.

Being in these places, seeing them first hand, was totally different from reading about Columbus and slavery in a history class.

Food-wise, meals were a treat. Although still a picky eater, I soon came to love the cook's callaloo fritters, ackee rice with salt fish, sweet plantains, and jerk chicken.

The only fly in the ointment was Dad. His mood, for whatever reason, turned increasingly sour day by day.

At the dinner table one evening, the young serving girl made the rounds with a salad for each setting.

Rain said, "Thank you, Doda."

Dad immediately turned on my sister: "Hey. *Respect!*"

"She *asked* me to call her Doda."

"*Don't talk back!*"

"But *Daddy*—"

Dad silenced her with a backhand slap across her face; she burst into tears and her nose started bleeding.

Dad and I glared at each other.

Clearly, he expected me, as the elder Pryor child, to take care of the situation.

I grabbed a napkin and led Rain to the bathroom, where I tilted her head back and pressed the napkin to her nose until she stopped bleeding.

I washed the blood from her face, cleaned her up, and we returned to the table.

It was quiet. Quiet and tense. And the main course was set.

Deboragh and Elizabeth had waited politely for Rain and me to return and sit down before eating; Dad was already chowing down.

I sat, put a napkin on my lap, and glanced at my plate. Rice-and-peas and some kind of odd-smelling stew.

I pointed: "What's that?"

"Eat it," Dad said, "it's good."

"What *is* it?"

"Rice-and-peas."

"I *know* that, I mean this *other* stuff."

"Jerk goat."

I was stunned. "*Goat?*"

"Eat it!"

"I'm not eating any goat!"

"I said *eat it!*"

"Kiss my ass!"

I threw my napkin down, stood, and stormed for the stairs.

Bam! Something hard struck the back of my head. *Owww!*

It was a salad bowl.

Yeah, Dad threw a salad bowl at me.

THE GRAND TOUR

For summer vacation, 1977, Dad took Deboragh, Rain (8), Elizabeth (10), and me (15) to Europe. As usual, we flew first class and stayed at the finest hotels.

In London, it was the Four Seasons. We hit Cartier's, where Dad bought me a watch, and gold jewelry for Deboragh and the girls.

He must have been able to bring his coke stash with him because he was in high spirits the entire trip.

Except for two incidents.

In Monte Carlo, Monaco, we stayed at the Hôtel Hermitage, on the Riviera. One morning, while Dad slept late, Deboragh took the girls and me down to the beach. This being the Riviera and very French-like, it was a topless beach. For Elizabeth, age ten, and Rain, soon to turn eight, topless was no big deal. For Deboragh, it was a huge deal: I mean, she had enormous breasts.

For a fifteen-year-old boy, it was a shock and a joy to see so many half-naked women cavort on the strand. It was another matter entirely to observe my father's girlfriend remove her bikini top and expose her boobs. I tried not to stare.

Back in our hotel suite, Dad asked if I had a good time at the beach. I dutifully reported what I'd seen and experienced. He was astounded that I'd looked at Deboragh's bare breasts and gave me a generous whupping for it. I knew it would be a waste of breath to proclaim my innocence, to complain that he should blame Deboragh. *She* should get the whupping.

The other incident occurred in Paris.

We stayed at the George V, a five-star deluxe hotel in the heart of town. One day after lunch at an outdoor café, Deboragh and Dad decided to spend the afternoon at the Louvre. My sisters and I weren't much interested in seeing the Mona Lisa, so we took a taxi back to the hotel.

At the front desk I got the key to our suite. Elizabeth and I wanted to stop in at the gift shop for dessert treats, but Rain started whining that she wanted to go up to the suite *now*.

Elizabeth and I were plenty annoyed, but to avoid a scene in the lobby we headed for the elevator.

We were silent on the ride up. As soon as we reached our floor, Elizabeth and I ran down the hall to our suite.

By the time Rain got there Elizabeth and I were inside with the door locked.

Rain proceeded to pound on the door and yell.

Inside the suite, Elizabeth and I ignored her, choosing instead to admire a painting that hung on the living room wall, one we'd never paid a mind to before, an oil color of the Tuileries Garden.

Elizabeth said, "Weren't we were there the day before yesterday?"

"Uh-huh. Dad bought us all ice cream."

The pounding on the door was hard to ignore, but I continued, "On the plane coming over, I read that French ice cream is made with cream and eggs, but American ice cream doesn't have eggs. It's with cream, milk, and sugar. Did you know that?"

"No. Interesting."

Suddenly, the pounding on the door stopped.

Elizabeth and I looked at each other, curious.

I went to the door, unlocked and opened it, and peered down the hall. Rain was crouched down behind an antique settee, her panties pulled down, peeing on the lavish carpet.

As soon as she was done I dragged her into the suite and spanked her butt.

When Dad got back, she told Dad on me.

I got whupped for that.

Then Elizabeth got whupped for her part in locking Rain out of the suite.

Then Rain got whupped for peeing in the hall.

In his comedy routine, Dad says he never whupped his kids because he didn't want them to get fucked up. Like him.

That gets a big laugh from everyone, except us Pryor kids.

ADAPTATION

The summer before my sophomore year in high school Dad bought Mom a new house in a subdivision called Rolling Acres.

That meant I would start the school year at Richwoods High School instead of Peoria Heights.

The change was abrupt and unsettling. Neither Mom nor Dad asked me in advance, "How would you feel about moving to the suburbs and switching schools?"

My opinion about a matter crucial to my existence was irrelevant. I had no more say than a piece of furniture.

On top of that, though Richwoods was more diverse than Peoria Heights HS, it was much larger. I knew no one there and missed the few pals I had at Peoria Heights. I felt, once again, like an outsider: removed, estranged, isolated.

In class, I barely paid attention; mostly, I daydreamed and doodled.

Homework assignments were sloppy; term papers, slapdash.

My grades slipped.

Nor had I any interest in extra-curricular activities, like chorus or drama.

In June, my final report card displayed mediocre grades. Yes, I would advance to my junior year in September, but barely.

SHRINKAGE 101

Ever since I was twelve, I had recurring nightmares. Generally, they involved some situation where I was helpless in the face of sexual molestation. Often it was by the hands of people who, in real life, I knew meant me no harm.

In my junior year those nightmares turned to night-terrors and I often woke up screaming.

Mom, aside from holding and comforting me when my screams woke her, was at a loss about what else to do.

School was a disaster.

In my younger days I'd been a math whiz; my wizardry tapered off when we hit fractions and decimals. Now, I was required to take geometry in order to graduate. I saw no earthly reason why I would ever, in my entire life, need to know geometry. In class I spaced out and rarely turned in homework assignments.

My final report card said that if I wanted to advance to my senior year I would have to attend summer school.

At Central High. With the rest of the dummies.

I started summer school.

One afternoon early in July, when I got home from a make-up class in geometry, Mom was in the backyard wearing overalls and washing windows.

"Hi, Richie."

"Hi."

"How was school?"

I rattled off, "A squared plus b squared equals c squared."

"Huh?"

"The hypotenuse of a right triangle, squared, is equal to the sum of the squares of the two legs."

She observed me for a minute.

"Pythagorean Theorem," I added, my voice quavering.

"Richie," she said gently, "why don't you change into some old clothes and help me wash the windows."

Instead, I burst into tears. It was worse than when I ran away from home, with *don't nobody loves me, don't nobody care* playing on endless loop in my mind.

I cried for hours, inconsolable.

This time I wasn't a child hiding out in Grandma Marie's station wagon. I was sixteen, and clearly suffering some kind of mental breakdown.

Mom consulted with her sister, Aunt Angie, and they decided to take me to St. Francis Hospital, where I was born, and which was now a major medical center with its very own psychiatric floor.

I was admitted, taken to the eighth-floor psycho ward, and assigned to a sweet, kind, understanding therapist, let's call her Dr. Young. She assured me that our therapy sessions were strictly confidential, so I poured my heart out: school problems, night-terrors, *when I was twelve* shit, tighty-whities in the Sears Roebuck catalogue, everything I could think of.

Mom visited daily. On one visit she asked me about Armando.
What?

Dr. Young had blabbed to my mother everything I revealed in confidence.

I was furious.

In consequence of Dr. Young's betrayal I shut down, refusing to talk to anyone, refusing to eat, and, finally, becoming disruptive on the ward. "Acting out," Dr. Young called it.

My father called and let me know that he'd spoken with Mom, spoken with Dr. Young, and if I didn't cool it the hospital would assign me to the Zeller Zone.

The Zeller Zone.

That meant the Insane Asylum.

I cooled it and was released the next day.

NO MORE WHUPPINGS

I spent the rest of that summer in Los Angeles at the Parthenia house. It was an estate Dad bought that was formerly owned by somebody-or-other and had a guest house where I took up residence.

Mornings, Dad hired a tutor to catch me up in school.

Afternoons, I worked in his office in the main house, reading screenplays for films under consideration.

One day, David Banks, his producer, asked me to please bring him a coffee from the kitchen.

I had another two pages to go. I said, "Hang on, David, let me just finish this."

Dad said, "You heard him, Richard. Put the fuckin' script down and go get him a coffee."

"I got one more page. As soon as I finish the mother-fucker, I'll get his fuckin' coffee."

Dad walked over to me, his temper rising.

I stood, thinking *I'm seventeen, too fucking old for this shit.*

I faced him and braced myself.

Sure enough, he punched me in the chest, hard.

I didn't budge, not an inch.

His jaw dropped open. He looked at his fist, at my chest, at me.

"Shit," he said, "*mother-fucker.*"

And that was the last time he laid a hand on me.

CLAP FOR RICHARD!

1980.

Finally, my senior year of high school.

For a pre-graduation present Dad bought me a car—a Pontiac Trans Am.

The gay cruising area in Peoria was the Riverfront. I'd drive down there in my hot Trans Am and pick up guys. Usually, older guys.

For the most part, they were very sweet men. In fact, some days my mother would find on the front porch, a cute coffee mug with my name on it, or, this one time, an adorable little teddy bear with a pink bowtie.

"Mom, I have no idea who left that teddy bear. Oh wait, there's this girl in my class who kinda has a crush on me. Should I give it back to her?"

"No, that's okay."

I couldn't tell her that the gifts were tokens of appreciation from men I'd had sex with. The fear of how she would react was way too great: that she would know how different I was and, as a result, would withdraw her love.

So I kept my secret, with one little scare.

I was in my room doing homework. I went to the bathroom to pee. *Ouch.*

I went down to the kitchen.

"Mom? My penis burns when I pee."

Next morning she drove me to the clinic.

The doctor brought me into an examining room, stuck a Q-tip into my dick—*OWWWW!*—and examined what came out on the cotton.

I pulled my pants back up and followed him back to the waiting room. He took Mom and me into his office and sat us down.

"Mrs. Price, your son has a venereal disease."

"*What?*"

"Gonorrhea."

"That's impossible. He's never had sex."

She glanced over at me. I shook my head. *"No! Never!"*

The doctor disregarded my disclaimer. "It's important," he told my mother, "that we get a list of everyone Richard has had sexual contact with."

"I *told* you, he *hasn't had any* sexual contacts. If he has a venereal disease, he must have picked it up from a toilet seat."

The doctor looked from Mom to me and back to her. He realized he wasn't going to get anywhere with either of us, so he just sighed and wrote out a prescription.

I took the pills, peed orange for a few days, and that was that. No more clap.

A HOT TIME IN LOS ANGELES

Dad came to Peoria to attend my high school graduation.

Although I was thrilled that he came, his presence at the event was a major distraction. The parents of my graduating class were more focused on Dad than on their own children. Lines formed for autographs. Cameras that were brought to take photos of happy high school kids receiving their diplomas were constantly focused on my father. I felt terrible for my fellow grads.

A week later, Tuesday, June ninth, I was in my Pontiac Trans Am cruising around, when the news came on the radio: Richard Pryor set fire to himself.

Mom, Uncle Dicky, and I were immediately on a flight to Los Angeles.

In the hospital, the Sherman Oaks Burn Center, we sat with him all through visiting hours. His head was heavily bandaged and he was heavily sedated. Whenever he moved you could see flakes of his skin shed onto the sheets.

It was horrible. I kept thinking, *There's no way he's gonna come out of this.*

In the waiting room, me and my cousin Denise, who lived in Los Angeles, read through Dad's fan mail. There was a photo of us doing that, which ran in the newspapers.

One funny moment in that nightmare: Mom, Shelley, Elizabeth's mother, Maxeine, and Deboragh were in the waiting room. Dr. Grossman, the surgeon who treated my father, came in and said, "Mrs. Pryor?"

All the women stood up.

Dad would later joke about it in one of his routines.

With expert care from Dr. Grossman, and a strong will to survive, Dad got better every day.

(The hospital has since been renamed: It's now the Grossman Burn Center. Dr. Grossman's son, Paul, also a plastic surgeon, is a Facebook friend of mine. Hi, Paul!)

Denise and me laughing over Dad's fan mail.

BUSTED

While Dad was in the hospital, getting better by the day, I stayed at the Parthenia guest house and cruised around town in one of Dad's cars, picking up guys and bringing them back to my abode.

This one time I picked up two cute dudes, actor/models, and brought them home for a threesome.

Four days later, I went out to buy breakfast for us.

When I returned my new roommates were frantically cleaning up the place.

I was astounded.

You see, back home in Peoria, Mom was always at me: "Richie, make up your bed! Richie, wash the dishes! Richie, take out the trash and sweep the floor!"

But here at Dad's, there was always a housekeeper to do that stuff. Hence, my astonishment at the guys cleaning.

"Like, what are you *doing?*" I asked.

"You haven't seen her?"

"Seen who?"

Right on cue, Patricia Von Heitman opened the door and popped her head into the room.

"Richard Junior," she said. "Your father wants to speak to you on the telephone. *Now.*"

Later on, I pieced together what happened. Unbeknownst to me, Dad was trying to sell the house, and while I was out shopping for breakfast some potential buyers came to look the place over. Patricia showed them around and when they got to the guest house, guess what they saw? Two naked guys fucking on my bed.

As soon as I got on the phone, Dad jumped right in.

"Are you gay?"

I went into total denial, sobbing, bawling, defending: "*Dad*, how can you *say* that!"

"Because *there's two naked guys fucking in your bed!*"

I'M NOT GAY, DAD!

Right after the *two naked guys fucking in your bed* incident, I set out to show Dad, to show the world, that I wasn't gay. I had just been, you know, *experimenting*.

To establish my heterosexual credentials, I embarked on an affair with a woman, Diane Collins. I was 18 and fresh out of high school, she was 27 and recently separated from her husband.

One morning, said husband showed up and banged on the front door. You can't believe how fast I snatched my clothing and escaped out a window.

Despite that near-disaster, I was still determined to prove that the gay thing was strictly a phase, a passing fancy. Deep down inside, I was totally straight and manly.

But how could I demonstrate my manliness?

The answer became obvious.

IN THE NAVY, IN THE NAVY

What could be more straight and manly than military service?

Eighteen and fresh out of high school, I enlisted in the Navy.

Mom wasn't thrilled, worried sick that America would go to war with some country and I'd be shipped there.

But no, we were between Vietnam and Iraq.

I was assigned to an aircraft carrier, the USS America.

Soon I learned that my fellow semen—oops, sorry, I meant sea-men—called our ship the Miss America.

Cue the Village People.

In the Navy

Come on, protect the mother land

In the Navy

Come on and join your fellow man

Yep, I joined my fellow man.

Men.

Many men.

When you're out at sea for five months at a time you develop the equivalence of cabin fever. The Miss America became *The Love Boat*. And the funny thing is, while there were a lot of gays on the ship, there were also a lot of straight men who were oh-so-willing to accept blow jobs from their fellow swabs, or—and I swear I witnessed this more than once—shove a butter-knife handle up their butt, in a stall in the head, with the door open.

That said, life aboard ship was hunky-dory. (It's a Navy expression meaning all is groovy. It derives from Honki-Dori Street in Okinawa, Japan, a street lined with establishments that cater to sailors on leave: bars, tattoo parlors, and whorehouses.)

We gay tars knew each other, of course. We even published a newspaper, *The Diva Gazette*. The articles were written and submitted under pseudonyms. Mine was "Unique."

Typical *Diva Gazette* reportage:

Ahoy, mate!

GAY-BASHED IN PANAMA
(Dateline: Panama City)
While emerging from a Panama City gay bar at three a.m., our very own Miss Juliette was savagely attacked by a teen gang of homophobes and beaten so bad she was returned to the ship in an ambulance. She's now in the medical unit. Flowers and psychedelics would be much appreciated.

Or:

THE VIRGIN ISLANDS POOP-SCOOP
(Dateline: Charlotte Amalie)
Miss Unique, your intrepid reporter, arrived at her swank hotel room to relieve Miss Buddyfuck, who was due back at the ship by 0800 hours, and found the housekeeper in the room, changing the linens and all in a tizz about suspicious stains on the sheets.

"I don't know what you call this in *your* country," she griped, "but here we call it poo-poo."

First thing we did on shore leave was head straight to the gay night-life spots. We had a book that listed them, with addresses and specialties, in every major port in the world.

One night, me and the boys were in a gay bar in Edinburgh, Scotland knocking back shots of the country's finest hooch. There was a song on the juke box: "And I'm Telling You I'm Not Going," from the Broadway show *Dreamgirls*. I was three sheets to the wind and didn't need much encouragement. I stood up on a chair and lip-synched the song with over-the-top dramatic gestures.

At the conclusion I took a deep bow and was greeted by thunderous applause.

The next night, my pals and I were admitted free, and I was persuaded to bust loose again.

January 13, 1982 — the Hoist — Page 3

This Seaman Apprentice is 'Bustin' Loose'

When you're the relative of a famous celebrity, life can be an endless struggle for self-identity. Being referred to as "the son or daughter of..." is a fate that all children of celebrities face.

"When people find out that I'm Richard Pryor's son they automatically expect me to be able to tell jokes and make them laugh," says Seaman Apprentice Richard F. Pryor, Jr. "People expect me to live up to the same personality traits that made my father a star. They find it hard to believe that I'm my own person and not a carbon copy of my father.

"While other people see him as Richard Pryor the comedian and actor of motion pictures, I see him as any other normal person. Being the son of a famous performer can be a strange thing at times. It's amazing how many people want my autograph, even though I haven't done anything commercially big yet."

SA Pryor is quiet upon meeting others. "The first impression that people get of me is that I'm reclusive, but I'm usually that way with everyone, at least until I get to know them and can feel comfortable around them."

He is 19 years old and has set himself the goal of becoming a screen actor.

"I've been fortunate to get some behind-the-scenes work through my father. I worked as the production assistant on 'Bustin' Loose,' the movie that starred my father and Cicely Tyson. I am the assistant to the producer for my dad's newest film "Some Kind of Hero"which is due for release in June. I have a small, non-speaking part in that movie."

SA Pryor wants to start off his acting career by doing dramatic roles. Having already spent six months studying at the distinguished Lee Strasberg Theater Institute in Los Angeles, he anticipates a future that will start with serious roles and ultimately gravitate towards comedy.

Pryor, a native of Peoria, Ill. is also a song and dance man. While attending Peoria Heights High School he acted and was the lead dancer in "South Pacific." He was subsequently voted "most artistic" during his senior year.

"I was part of a small group of back dancers that performed with soul singer James Brown."

There is a great deal of artistic talent in SA Pryor. Besides acting, singing, and dancing, he does abstract sculpture, watercolors, writes scripts and poetry.

Individuality is something SA Pryor wants very much. His constant need to "be my own person and establish independence" led him to the Navy where he feels he is "already starting off at a good pace."

He graduated from RTC Company 265 on Dec. 31.

"Many of the guys in my recruit company asked me to autograph letters that they sent home. There were a few guys that wanted me to tell jokes. Some of them were disappointed if I turned them down. Of course they asked a lot of questions about my father's lifestyle on and off camera.

"My father and I are alike in many ways. People will find this hard to believe, but he's basically a quiet person."

SA Pryor wants to establish himself in the Navy's Personnelman rating. He has obligated himself to a four year contract and says that a career in the Navy is a real possibility for him.

Presently he is assigned to Seaman Apprenticeship Training here.

"I'm glad to be in the Navy because through it I can build myself up on an individual basis and better direct my life."

by JO3 Otis Zachary

The Hoist, *Jan. 13, 1982.*

Time for a Change?

I was stationed in our home port, Norfolk, Virginia. I had rented a nice little townhouse in Virginia Beach and tooled around town in the Trans Am Dad gave me.

But after three years at sea something changed in me: women began to look attractive.

Maybe it was three years of being cooped up with horny men sticking butter-knife handles up their ass.

One afternoon I was shopping in the Military Circle Mall and there was this cute young Southern girl working at the Cookie Shop.

Sonia.

We started talking; she reminded me of that Beach Boys song, "and those Southern girls with the way they talk, they knock me out when I'm down there."

Sonia had that southern accent; it knocked me out.

We fell in love.

She moved into my townhouse.

I met her family—a stunningly normal, freakishly all-American family unit, unlike anything I was used to.

Wow, I thought, *that's what I want, to be a part of that life, that stability.*

I asked her to marry me.

She said yes, and we planned for the wedding.

My gay shipmates were initially taken aback, but on recovery they all asked the same question: "Please, can I be the flower girl?"

WALLOPED

A week before the wedding, Sonia and I had a joint bachelor/bachelorette party in our townhouse.

A friend of Sonia's arrived with her fiancé, Winston.

Oh God, *Winston!*

Winston was, like, the most beautiful man I'd ever laid eyes on in my entire life, in person or in a movie.

I felt like Tony in *West Side Story* when he sees Maria for the first time. I wanted to run through the streets of Virginia Beach singing his name at the top of my lungs: "Win-*ston!* Win-*ston!* I'll never stop saying *Win*-ston!"

I tried not to obsess on him since he was straight and engaged to a girlfriend of Sonia's. And I reminded myself over and over that I was to be married in two days. To a lovely woman. The thought filled me with doom and despair. I contemplated various methods of suicide.

When the party ended Sonia and I were too tired to do anything more than fall asleep in the same bed.

The next afternoon, Dad flew in from Los Angeles.

We went out for dinner.

When drinks arrived Dad raised his glass of Courvoisier. "To a long, happy marriage. Or at least, longer than any of mine."

I raised my glass to clink, but my hand was trembling so bad half my gin-and-tonic sloshed onto the table.

"Nervous?" he asked. "Because that's normal."

I chugged down my drink and signaled for another round.

"Or is it something else?" he said.

"Something else."

The something else was Winston. Or actually, the *idea* of Winston.

"Okay, listen," he said, "don't do anything you're not ready to do."

"Uh-huh."

"Son, you do not have to get married."

"Really?"

"Really."

He reached into his shirt pocket and pulled out a folded check.

"Whatever you decide, either way, this is for you."

He handed me the check.

I unfolded it.

Pay to the order of Richard Pryor Jr.

Fifty thousand dollars.

FREE AGAIN

I called off the wedding.

Many of Sonia's friends and family could not be reached in time and showed up at the church eager to see our marriage—and meet the world-famous actor/comedian Richard Pryor. Some guests had already flown in from points distant.

There was widespread anger, tears, and recriminations.

I felt awful: guilt-stricken and miserable; a low-life, a cad, a rotten scoundrel.

On the other hand, I had that $50,000.

First thing, I went to a car dealership and bought a cute little Mazda RX-7.

Alas, it had a stick shift, which I couldn't drive, so I bumpety-bumped my baby off the lot, trying to put it in gear.

To complete the picture: a Michael Jackson zipper jacket.

That's either Michael Jackson or me. Hard to tell in this blurry pic.

50 GRAND

After the wedding debacle I started flying from Norfolk up to New York every week or so with a few of my Navy pals: David, from personnel; Kevin, who worked with me in the dispersing office; and Scott, from aviation maintenance.

With the sizeable chunk of cash that remained from Dad's $50,000 non-wedding present, I paid for everything: the flights, the hotel, and all expenses.

We invariably stayed in a penthouse suite at the Grand Hyatt on 42nd Street. The first time we checked in I asked the bellhop if he might be able to score us some "party favors."

"Sure, man," he said. I handed him two hundred-dollar bills. Within the hour he returned with a baggie of white powder. Cocaine. I was expecting marijuana, but hey. I thanked him and gave him a fifty-dollar tip.

I'd never done coke before, but I'd certainly seen my father do it often enough to know the ritual. I dumped some powder onto the glass-topped desk, chopped it fine with the edge of a credit card, and laid out eight lines for me and my mates. A rolled-up hundred-dollar bill in lieu of a straw, and we were in business.

My first time doing cocaine I immediately knew it would not be the last time.

Several snorts later, we hit the town.

First stop was a head shop, where I bought one of those little screw-on vials with a tiny spoon attached by a chain to the cap.

Next, we hit a gay bar. Gin-and-tonics all around. I went to the restroom and transferred my cocaine stash from the baggie to my new head-shop purchase. And took another bump.

A second gay bar, this one with a live drag show, guys in gorgeous gowns and wigs lip-synching to Grace Jones and Madonna.

As I watched the performers my mind went back to my smash performance in Edinburgh, when I stood on a chair and lip-synched

"And I'm Telling You I'm Not Going," and I thought, *I could do this drag thing!*

Later, we hit the Paradise Garage for some serious dancing. The Garage—or *Gay*rage— had the best sound system in town, and the DJ, Larry Levan, mixed pop songs by the Clash and the Police with gay disco anthems like "I'm Coming Out" and "It's Raining Men." The Paradise Garage sound became known as House Music.

As the night dwindled down we moseyed over to the Meatpacking District which, in those days, was literally a meatpacking district, not like now, a popular dining and tourist destination. There were no expensive restaurants or designer boutiques. After working hours the neighborhood was deserted, unlit and bleak. A perfect location for the dark events unfolding inside private clubs and unlocked meat trucks.

For example, you'd hear about a certain tucked-away place, get the address, locate an unmarked door, and knock. A doorman would observe you through a keyhole. If you didn't look like an undercover cop he'd let you in: pay admission, and then down a flight of rickety stairs you go into a dimly lit dungeon. There you could watch naked guys chained to a wall getting whipped. Guys fucking, guys getting fist-fucked, threesomes and foursomes. You were welcome to participate.

When we were ready to call it a night we emerged, eyes blinking against the morning light. By daytime the area was a bustle of activity: men in white blood-stained smocks unloading animal carcasses from trucks and carrying them into shops to be butchered.

That was our typical 36 hours on the town.

Not exactly Frank Sinatra, Gene Kelly, and Ann Miller.

A STAR IS BORN!

After that first weekend in New York I couldn't get the thought out of my head: *I could do this drag thing!*

When we returned to Norfolk I checked out the gay clubs there that had drag shows. The thought in my head grew stronger. *I could KILL at this thing.*

On our next trip to New York, besides the Grand Hyatt penthouse suite, the cocaine, the drag shows, the Paradise Garage, the dungeons, I added in a side trip to buy an outfit: a wig; a dress; matching coat, hat, and luggage; six-inch fuck-me pumps; and stockings. Yes, stockings. In the pursuit of artistic perfection, I would shave my legs.

My first performance was at the Cue Club, a Norfolk gay hangout which held a weekly competition based on TV's *The Gong Show*. I performed my standard Jennifer Holiday number and nailed it.

My chief rival in the contest was Miss Katrina Gail Phillips.

When she was announced as the winner the audience booed and threw drinks. A near riot.

In the dressing room I asked Miss Katrina Gail Phillips why she thought she beat me.

She said, "Sweetie, when you walked, your toenails scraped the dance floor. You need a pedicure."

Bull shit. I'm way too OCD for my toenails to grow so long that they'd scrape the floor.

Still, runner-up for my first shot at stardom was very encouraging.

On our next trip to New York I went on a spree: dresses, a gown, more wigs, more pumps, and make-up, tons of make-up.

Back in Norfolk, I started doing drag shows on a regular basis at the Cue Club and The Oar House, a hangout frequented by gay shipmen.

I became so popular and in demand that I'd finish a performance in one club or bar, then rush off to another venue for another performance.

Standard pay was $50 per show plus tips. Gin-and-tonic money.

Between fun-packed weekends in New York City and drag shows in Norfolk, I was a happy camper.

A Sight to Behold

On one of my New York City excursions, near the end of a long night, I stopped into a Greenwich Village after-hours gay bar, and guess who I saw?

Remember Harry Price, Mom's second husband who would get so mad at her that he'd bash her head against a wall?

Yep, my evil step-dad cruising the room.

My *queer* evil stepdad.

I turned around and high-tailed it.

OUT OF THE NAVY, OUT OF THE NAVY

Of course, I was still in the Navy, which meant going to sea.

A day before we were scheduled to ship out, a sailor—let's call him Janus—boarded the Miss America.

This was in the era of "Don't Ask, Don't Tell," but Janus was so flamboyantly swish it was a miracle he hadn't been discovered.

Janus wasted no time in getting buddy-buddy with the gay contingent, although his mannerisms put us off.

And then one day, *poof*, he was gone.

Next day, I was called down to the ship's Naval Investigative Service office. In the waiting room were two friends, members of the *Diva Gazette* crew.

Uh-oh.

The first of the crew was ordered into the hearing room. Ten minutes later, he emerged, pale-faced. Without a look in our direction, he headed straight for the door and was out.

My second friend took even less time. When he emerged he looked at me and burst into tears. Then he too ran out.

Last, me.

Inside the hearing room were three stern-looking Naval officers sitting stiffly erect behind a long table. Let's call them Larry, Curly, and Mo.

On command, I raised my right hand and swore to tell the truth.

Then they jumped in.

Curly: "Seaman Pryor, did you engage in acts of sodomy and fellatio with Seaman A?"

He mentioned a seaman with whom I'd engaged in frequent acts of sodomy and fellatio.

So much for "Don't Ask, Don't Tell."

Me: "*No*, sir."

Larry: "Seaman Pryor, did you engage in acts of sodomy or fellatio with Seaman B?

Another sodomized and fellated friend.

Larry: "Seaman Pryor?"

"No, sir, I did not engage in acts of sodomy or fellatio with Seaman B."

Mo: "Seaman Pryor, did you engage in acts of sodomy or fellatio with *any* crew member aboard the USS America?"

"No, sir, never."

Curly: "Pryor, have you ever referred to this ship as the *Miss America*?"

"No, sir."

Curly: "Pryor, when the ship was docked in Edinburgh, Scotland, did you attend a gay bar, where you—" He glanced at his notes. "Where you lip-synched to a song, 'And I'm Telling You I'm not Going?'"

"A gay bar? You mean, a bar frequented by homosexuals?"

Curly wasn't having any of it. He handed me a copy of *The Diva Gazette*.

Curly: "Pryor, let me remind you that you're under oath, and lying to this tribunal is a federal crime."

"Yes, sir. Thank you, sir."

Curly: "You're dismissed. Wait outside."

I waited outside. Fifteen minutes later, I was summoned back in.

Mo handed me an official-looking paper and said, "Pryor, you're being discharged."

"What? *Why?*"

All three of them gave me a raised-eyebrow look.

Mo continued: "Pack up and be ready to leave at 1200 hours."

"But we're a thousand miles out. What am I supposed to do, swim ashore?"

"Dismissed, Pryor."

I left, so shocked that it didn't dawn on me till I was back on deck and saw those rows of A-7 Corsair II fighter jets: *We're on an aircraft carrier, they're gonna fly me home.*

They did.

At noon, I climbed into one of those sexy A-7 Corsairs, snapped on a seat belt and shoulder harness and, seconds later, was pancaked against my seatback by a G4 transverse thrust as the jet shot into the air.

At supersonic speed, we arrived in Jacksonville, Florida in no time.

A vehicle waited to take me to a nice hotel, courtesy of the U.S. Navy.

That night over drinks, David, my friend from personnel, told me there was an order from Jacksonville HQ to treat me with kid gloves. I figured they didn't do that with every gay seaman who got axed. No, they probably just didn't want a lot of hoopla about an Administrative Discharge for the son of Richard Pryor.

Thanks, Dad!

Hello, Mother. Hello, Father. Guess what?

From Jacksonville, they flew me to Norfolk, where I still had the townhouse.

I stayed in and stewed on the fact that I was drummed out of the service for being homosexual. I decided to clue my parents in; clear the decks; set the record straight, so to speak.

First up, Dad.

As usual, a woman I didn't know answered the phone. "Pryor residence."

"Hi, this is Richard Jr., may I speak to my father please?"

"One moment."

Dad got on the phone.

"Son, you okay?"

"Yeah, I just want to tell you something."

"Hang on."

I heard the thunk of a phone set down on a hard surface and then a distinct *ffffffffffffft*, a sound I recognized as a line of cocaine being sucked into a nostril.

Then another one for balance: *ffffffffffffffft*.

"Okay, I'm here. What's up?"

"I'm no longer in the Navy."

"Oh? I thought you had another year."

"They kicked me out."

"Mother-fucker! Congratulations!"

Dad had been kicked out of the Army.

"They throw you in the stockade first?"

Before they discharged him, he was locked in a military prison for a year.

"In the Navy they call it the brig, Dad. But no, they didn't throw me in the brig."

"Uh-huh, so wha'd ya do, stab some racist mother-fucker?"

Dad was imprisoned and discharged for stabbing a guy who made racist remarks.

I took a deep breath and let it out. Then said, "They found out I'm gay."

Silence.

I braced myself for the explosion.

Instead, there was that thunk of the phone set down again, and then another *fffffffffffft*.

I listened for the second snort.

No second snort.

"Dad?"

"Took the fuckin' U.S. Navy three fuckin' years to figure that out? *Damn*."

"So, you're okay wit it?"

"Uh, listen to me now . . . not everyone . . . needs to know . . . everything you do. Ya dig?"

"You mean, don't tell Mom?"

Another thunk, another *fffffffffffft*. The other nostril.

"And whatever you do . . . *whatever you fuckin' do* . . . do it *all the way* . . . the best you can . . . Not . . . not half-assed . . . *Don't hold back* . . . . Know what I mean?"

Actually, no, I had no idea what he meant. I chalked it up to well-intentioned parental advice bursting from a location deep in my father's coke-addled brain.

"Thanks, Dad. I love you."

"Yeah, me too."

We hung up and I breathed a sigh of relief. The hard part was over.

Mom, I knew, would be easy. For one thing, she must already suspect. There was that period where she called me Lionel, after her swishy hairdresser. And the girlish gifts that my male admirers left on the porch, like that pink teddy bear. And the basement all-male party.

Oh, and surely she had discovered by now that you don't catch gonorrhea from a toilet seat and, if I had been having sex with a girl, I wouldn't have been so vehement in proclaiming my virginity.

Bottom line, no one knew me better than my mom. She *must* have discovered my secret.

The good news was she loved me unconditionally, no matter what craziness I was up to.

Yeah, telling Mom I was gay would be a piece of cake.

I dialed her number.

"Hello?"

"Hi, Mom, it's Richie."

"*Richie!* You okay?"

I'm sure there's a reason why both my parents, whenever they speak to me, the first thing out of their mouth is, "Are you okay?"

"I'm fine, Mom. But listen, I'm not in the Navy any more."

"Thank God! I was so worried."

Worried the U.S.A. would go to war and the Miss America sent into battle.

"But listen. The reason is, they kicked me out."

"Why?"

"They found out I'm gay."

"What? I don't understand."

"I'm gay, Mom. Homosexual."

"*Noooooooooooooo!*"

Oh shit, I totally misjudged this one.

Between the sobs and wails, she managed, "*Are you sure?*"

"Yeah."

"*Where did I go wrong?*"

"It's not your fault. It's no one's fault."

Another round of sobs and wails. Probably some gnashing of teeth.

"Mom, I gave notice on my townhouse, I'll be back in Peoria first of the month. Okay if I stay with you?"

"Of course! Only . . .uh . . . maybe don't tell anybody else about . . . your condition."

"My homosexual condition."

"It'll be our little secret. Don't even tell your dad, okay?"

"Mom—"

"—Promise me!"

How funny. Both Mom and Dad with the same thought, the same pearls of wisdom. Birds of a feather. No wonder they flocked together.

"Richie? Promise?"

"Yes, Mom. Promise."

ZOOM ZOOM

I mastered the art of shifting gears. On the Mazda, at least, not in life—not yet, not by a long shot.

Since the Sonia wedding fiasco I'd become good friends with Winston. I gave him $100 to move and park the Trans Am every couple of days until I could figure out what to do with it.

I packed the Mazda with all my clothing plus the drag-show costumes I'd bought in New York and headed into the Heartland.

Virginia. . . .

West Virginia. . . .

Driving all night.

Hillbilly music on the radio, Dolly Parton singing, appropriately enough, "I Really Don't Want to Know." Dolly non-stop, till I knew all the words and sang along with her: "Even if I ask you/Darlin' don't confess."

Ohio. . . .

Indiana. . . .

Finally, Illinois.

I drove straight through, one fell swoop; 17 hours, with pee breaks and food stops only when I needed to gas up. All the way I kept thinking, *I'm 22 years old, I've been in the United States Navy, traveled the world, performed in drag shows, and watched men fist-fuck. And now I will be doomed to a closeted existence in Peoria with my mother, sworn to keep my sexual preference "our little secret."*

HOME

For a week it was great to reconnect with old friends and family. Then, just as I feared, it was stifling.

The only glimmer of hope was Larry, a dude I'd been very friendly with in high school, and now. . . Hey-hey, whu'd'ya say—Larry turned out to be gay.

Larry Woods.

He was White (of course), short and compact, maybe five-foot-six, with dirty-blond hair, blue eyes, an infectious smile, and a huge cock.

We started dating.

Larry was younger than me and still lived at home with his father and kid brother. We couldn't carry on our affair at his house, and I definitely couldn't bring him home to Mom, so romantic opportunities were few and far between. We explored sex in the Mazda. After one or two attempts I remembered from my high school cruising days that the Trans Am was more suited to that purpose.

I called Winston to see if he knew anyone headed to Chicago who would drive my car to Peoria, and then I'd drive them the rest of the way to Chicago. As soon as he answered the phone and I said, "Hey, it's Richard," he got real quiet.

"Winston?"

"Shit, I'm sorry, man, I screwed up."

"Huh?"

"I got side-tracked."

"Pardon?"

"I forgot to move the car."

"And?"

"It got towed."

"Shit!"

"I'm sorry."

"Where is it now?"

"In the pound. It's three hundred dollars to get it out. Plus a fine for the parking ticket, another hundred."

"*Fuck!*"

"I don't have the dough. I'm sorry, man."

Being a life-long fuck-up myself, I wasn't about to deliver him a lecture on responsibility.

"Don't worry about it," I said.

He promised that if I sent him the money he'd drive it to Peoria himself.

I said I'd get back to him.

The truth was, I'd spent the last of Dad's fifty grand on the drive here. I didn't have four hundred dollars. And I was too embarrassed to ask Mom or Dad for the money.

For all I know, that Trans Am is still parked in a Norfolk impoundment lot, rotting away.

BOOM!

To lift my spirits I decided to have a small soiree. I mean, I was a grown-up, an adult, I had every right to throw a party.

Of course, I scheduled it for a weekday afternoon, when Mom was at work.

My little shindig would be in the basement, where we had a wet bar, a stereo, and some nice furniture.

I invited Larry and a few guys we knew from school or the neighborhood.

Word got out; 20-30 guys arrived.

As host, bartender, and DJ, I had my hands full. The music was LOUD, the booze flowed, joints were passed, guys were dancing and making out. It was a very successful soiree.

Until I heard my mother's voice from the top of the basement stairs cutting through the music. "*Richard?*"

Oh shit.

I ran up to stairs to meet her.

She stood on the top step.

"What the *hell* is going on?"

"Nothing. I invited a few friends over—"

"—*Who gave you permission!?*"

"You're mad at me."

"*Yes!*"

"Okay. Hit me."

"*What?*"

"Go ahead, get it out of your system. Hit me."

I thrust my chest out and braced myself, like I did with Dad when he punched me in the chest.

Mom punched me in the face, right on the chin.

Boom!

I fell backward and tumbled head over heels down the basement stairs.

The fall didn't hurt me, I was too drunk and relaxed.

I got up, brushed myself off, and climbed the stairs.

Mom was gone, probably in her bedroom. She must have been *really* mad—she didn't even stick around to check that I wasn't injured.

LARRY

Living the closeted life with my mother was so frustrating that every once in a while I'd get a hair up my ass and just get in my car, drive to Los Angeles for a few days, live it up at Dad's, and drive back to Peoria.

Or Purgatory, as I now called it.

Eventually I persuaded Larry to move to Los Angeles with me.

Yay!

I sold the Mazda to buy plane tickets and, in August 1984 we departed Purgatory.

Dad more-or-less accepted that I was gay, but I wasn't about to rub it in his face. I stayed in the guest house, Larry stayed with a friend.

Dad gave me a job at his company, Indigo Productions, where I assisted his accountant, Jenny Ford.

He also insisted that I see a shrink, which he would pay for. Based on my high school experience with Dr. Young, I was apprehensive, but Dad was less concerned about my homosexuality than he was about my tendency to withdraw, feel isolated, and become depressed.

My new shrink prescribed anti-depressant pills to be taken at any time those feelings arose.

In December two other friends from Peoria arrived: Chris "Chrissy" Wheeler and Ricky Woods (not related to Larry, though they called each other cousins). In high school they'd been close friends with Larry and me.

Dad found us an apartment on Balboa, right around the corner from his house and office on Parthenia. I could walk to work, a rarity in Los Angeles.

None of us had cars; we took taxis to get around, which in LA is very expensive. So we mostly hung out at the apartment.

Eventually I saved enough money to put a down payment on a new Volkswagen Cabriolet. We had wheels. A communal car.

Within a year it became apparent that Larry was losing interest in me. We'd be out at a bar or club and I'd see him flirt with another guy, right under my nose. It drove me nuts, but confrontation was not in my vocabulary.

I consulted with Chrissie and Ricky.

Ricky said I was being paranoid, that Larry adored me.

Chrissie shrugged. He didn't want to get involved. That told me a lot.

Events came to a boil late one night when I woke up and Larry wasn't there. I felt certain he had gone off with Jay, a guy who'd been partying in the apartment with us earlier in the evening.

I couldn't go back to sleep. I got dressed and waited outside for Larry to come home.

After a while he pulled up in my VW, parked, got out, and, when he saw me, stood there and stared.

"Where you been?" I demanded.

"I drove Jay back to his place."

"Jay has his own car."

"I mean, we went for a drink. You were crashed out, we didn't wanna wake Sleeping Beauty."

"*Sleeping Beauty?*"

He shrugged.

I pressed on. "And after the drink?"

"He told me he had some blow at his place, so I followed him home."

"And fucked him?"

He just stood there and grinned. Then he headed for the apartment.

I grabbed his arm, spun him around, and proceeded to beat the shit out of him.

LA VIDA LOCA

In the morning I felt horrible about hurting him.

Sure, I could intellectually justify what I'd done, tell myself he deserved a beat-down for being such a shit.

The justification didn't help. I was waylaid by the Four Horsemen of the Emotional Apocalypse: Guilt, Self-loathing, Depression, and Suicidal Thoughts.

I promised Larry I would never ever hit him again.

He promised never to cheat on me again.

We had make-up sex.

It didn't take long for it to go downhill.

Is there a Dolly Parton song called "Promises Made, Promises Broken"?

Maybe it was Los Angeles: the weather, the palm trees, the SoCal do-your-thing-man vibe.

Larry felt free to do his thing.

And I became an uptight mother-fucker.

Ricky continued to pooh-pooh my jealousy.

Chrissie couldn't handle the tension and returned to Peoria.

One morning, when Larry came home after being out all night, I exploded again and pounded away at him.

We made up, but seeing his split lip, swollen cheekbone, and black eye, I was again awash in guilt and self-loathing.

I wanted to call Dad, but what could I tell him? "Dad, my boy-friend cheats on me and then I want to kill him."

He'd understand the I-want-to-kill-him part, definitely, but the my-boyfriend part? Not so much.

And Mom? The last thing in the world she'd want to hear would be any sentence from me that contained "my boyfriend." Besides, I think she was still irked that I hadn't said goodbye to her when I left Peoria. She only found out I was gone after Larry and I arrived in Los Angeles and I called her.

No, there was no one I could turn to. For the umpteenth time in my life I felt totally isolated, totally alone.

By high noon three of the Four Horsemen rode up and dismounted: Guilt, Self-loathing, and Depression.

For brunch, the Fourth blew in: Sir Suicide.

I found the pills my shrink had prescribed for me. I had yet to take any. I read the label: Not to exceed two times in one day.

Great, I would swallow the entire bottle. Fuck it.

The thing is, I hated taking pills. They always got stuck under my tongue and I would have to drink, like, a gallon of water to wash a single pill down.

But I was determined.

I sat down in the kitchen with the vial of meds, a glass, and a pitcher of water. By the time I swallowed, one-by-one, a lot of pills, I had to run to the bathroom every two minutes to pee.

The medication kicked in, my depression gave way to elation, then giddiness, then the whirly-twirlies. The path from kitchen to bathroom and back became an exercise in navigation.

But after one such bathroom run, it suddenly struck me how devastating my death would be to the family.

Mom. Dad. Rain, Elizabeth, and Elanda. Aunt Angie.

Fuck, I can't do this.

I called my shrink.

"Richard, how many pills did you take?"

"Uh, I dunno."

"Did you start with a new bottle?"

"Uh-huh."

"Okay, count how many you have left.

I spilled the remaining pills onto the table and silently counted.

One Mississippi . . . .

Two Mississippi . . . .

Three Mississippi . . . .

(I remembered the first time I was drunk, in Peoria when I was three years old, with Mom and her friends.)

Four Mississippi . . . .

(In the park.)

Seven Mississippi . . . .

(I staggered around, dizzy and dazed.)

"Richard? You there?"

"Uh-huh."

"What are you doing?"

"Counting pills."

"Okay, what number are you up to?"

"Uh."

"Richard?"

"Uh-huh."

"How many?"

"I lost count."

"Start again."

"Yeah. Okay."

I had a brainstorm. I arranged the pills in rows instead of counting them one by one, I'd only count the pills in each row, then multiply by the number of rows. Like counting the stars on a U.S. flag: eight stars in each row, six rows, six times eight is 48. 48 stars=48 states.

Except wait, there are 50 states.

"Richard, count out loud."

"Okay. I'm gonna count by twos, it'll go faster."

"Fine. Out loud."

I began, moving two at a time, fast, so I wouldn't screw up again.

"Two four six eight ten twelve!"

"Twelve, you're sure."

"Pretty sure."

"Okay. There were thirty pills in the prescription, so you've taken eighteen."

"I gotta pee."

"Go pee. And throw the rest of the pills down the toilet."

"But then I won't have any. For my depression."

"Listen, I'm going to call your father's office and tell them to send someone over to look after you."

"I gotta pee real bad."

"Go pee, but don't leave the house."

Pretty soon Dad's accountant, Jenny Ford, arrived, packed a suitcase for me, and drove straight to the BHC Alhambra Hospital, a psychiatric clinic in the Valley. My shrink phoned ahead to make the reservation, and Jenny let them know my dad would be responsible for the bill.

I was quickly checked in, into a semi-private unit, where my roommate was a beautiful dark-haired boy with piercing blue eyes named Michael.

Ah, Michael.

During the day the patients did all kinds of psychologically healthful activities: private therapy, group therapy, exercise classes, yoga, lectures, art classes, and group walks.

But my real recovery took place at night, after lights-out: my beautiful roommate Michael and I went at it like beasts.

Life would have been perfect if only we had some drugs.

And then fate stepped in.

REMEMBER COUSIN DENISE?

On a typical sunny Southern California afternoon I was out with my group for a therapeutic stroll. We passed a suburban house, and there in the driveway was a station wagon, light blue with wood paneling. I would have recognized that mother-fucker anywhere. It's the one I locked myself in when I ran away from home and cried *Don't nobody loves me, don't nobody care.*

It had been Grandma Marie's. She gave it to Denise when Denise moved out here.

The last time I'd seen Denise was four years ago in the Sherman Oaks Burn Center after Dad set fire to himself and she and I read his fan mail.

Here's some Denise backstory:

She was Grandma Marie's granddaughter, grew up in Peoria, and attended a Catholic high school, the Academy of Our Lady. One evening she was home alone in Marie's house and a guy broke in and assaulted her. She twisted away and ran into the kitchen. He ran after her, but she made it to the breadbox, where Grandma Marie always kept a loaded pistol.

Denise grabbed the gun and aimed it at the guy. He turned and ran, she pulled the trigger. The bullet hit him in the back. He fell, paralyzed.

You'd see him sometimes, kneeling on a gurney, paddling down the Peoria sidewalks, begging for change.

Back to the present:

As soon as I saw that station wagon I broke from my group and knocked on her door.

"Richie! What a surprise, come in!"

"I can't right now, I'm with my group."

"Group?"

"From BHC Alhambra."

"Oh. You okay?"

"Better. In fact, I'm gonna be released in a few days."

"You need a place to stay?"

I hadn't thought about that. "Yeah. Kinda."

"Look, I always park in the driveway. We could fix the garage up, get you a bed and stuff, make it kinda homey, and you can live there till you're back on your feet."

"Wow, thanks!"

As soon as I was released we spent a day shopping for essentials and fixing up the garage.

I moved in, never suspecting that cousin Denise was a closet crack addict.

CRACKED

David, my friend from the Navy who had been part of my Norfolk-to-Manhattan debauchery gang, now lived in South Central Los Angeles. He visited me in my humble abode.

We laughed about fun times on the Miss America, the drag shows, the wild parties, the *Diva Gazette*.

At some point David pulled out a glass pipe and a Ziploc bag with little white rocks inside. Crack.

"Okay if I do a pipe?" he asked.

"Sure. As long as I can try it."

"Richard, this shit is totally addictive—and you got an addictive personality. Plus, you just got out of rehab."

"No, it wasn't rehab, it was a psychiatric institute."

"Great."

"Come on, just once. I can't get addicted on one pipe."

David sighed. "Okay, just one."

He placed a little bit of steel wool in the pipe bowl, took a rock from the plastic bag, and set it on top of the steel wool.

He lit a match and held it over the bowl, gently drawing on it to melt the crack. Then he gave me the pipe.

"When you inhale, hold it in for as long as you can. And then exhale slowly."

I anticipated that holding it down for a long time would make me cough, like marijuana. But it wasn't like weed at all. It was an overwhelming, incredible rush. An immediate high.

Yeah, I was addicted.

COPPING

It wasn't long before Denise and I became aware of our shared crack addiction.

Thereafter, we took turns copping.

One time, when it was my turn to score, I drove the station wagon to South Central.

It was always strange to drive that car because I'd spent so much time in it back in Peoria when it was Grandma Marie's, and now driving it on crack-buy missions.

South Central Los Angeles, as you may have heard if you listen to West Coast hip-hop, was not the best neighborhood in the world.

Typically I'd pull up to a certain corner, this little kid would saunter over, I'd give him money, he'd disappear into one of the abandoned houses that lined the block, and five minutes later he'd return with my order.

On this one occasion though, my usual kid wasn't there. Instead there were two kids, one big, one little.

As soon as they reached the car the big kid pulled a pistol from his belt and held it to my head.

"Your usual order?" he asked.

"Yes. Please."

He held out his hand and I gave him the money.

He passed the money to the little kid, who hurried off to the same abandoned house my former supplier had operated out of.

Meanwhile, with the gun still pointed at my head, the big kid said, "Change in management. From now on, you buy from me."

"Sure. Not a problem."

A minute later the little kid returned with my bag of crack.

They both turned and left, and I fled the scene like a speed-demon. At the stoplight on the corner, my foot shook so violently I could barely control the brake pedal.

I remember thinking, *Dear God, I can't take this shit. What am I doing with my life?*

Denise and I smoked crack all night.

I Know it's There

There comes a time in every addict's life when the cupboard is bare, when the plastic bag is utterly empty.

Is he worried?

Not at all.

He knows, without a doubt, that he has oh-so-cleverly stashed away a hit or three for just such a rainy day.

All he has to do now is remember where he stashed it. Of course, since he was stoned stupid when he hid it he has no idea where it is.

So he embarks on a search.

On this particular occasion I turned the garage upside down and inside out looking for my secret cache, while Denise watched me with growing skepticism.

See, Denise had been a crack addict far longer than me, and so had been through that whole I-know-it's-here-somewhere trip too many times.

My search continued. I dug through all my clothing. Who knows, maybe one time when I was totally baked I'd stuck a rock in a pocket for just such an occasion.

And sure enough, guess what!?

There in a jacket pocket, I struck gold. A smallish rock, yes, but enough to get us both off.

I displayed my treasure in triumph.

"Oh ye of little faith," I said.

We lit up and passed the pipe back and forth, smoking up a storm.

Pretty soon we looked at each other.

"Richie, you feel anything?"

"No. You?"

"No."

"What the hell!"

I turned my coat pocket inside out and took a closer look at the contents.

Then I remembered.

Two days ago I had an apple turnover for lunch. Now Denise and I were trying to get high by smoking the sugary glaze that had crumbled off the apple turnover.

Like Dave Chappelle says, "Everything is funny, until it happens to you."

FLOOR ON THE FOURTH

It was the Fourth of July weekend and I was dressed to the nines: white pants, white shirt, and white buck shoes. If you're old enough to remember him, imagine a spiffy African-American Pat Boone.

My Navy pal David was in my garage apartment and we decided to smoke a pipe before heading around the corner, where his friends were having a Southern-style July 4th barbecue: Ribs, burgers, mac-and-cheese, slaw, cornpone, deviled eggs, all that.

Of course, I never made it to the barbecue.

When I woke up the next morning—well, two-fifteen in the afternoon, to be precise—I was fully clothed and my beautiful white outfit was filthy.

I learned from David, who'd actually made it to the event, that I'd dropped a piece of rock on the floor and crawled around on my hands and knees looking for it until I passed out.

Happy Independence Day!

MOVING ON DOWN

In 1985 I was a production coordinator on *The Color Purple*.

The film was shot partly in North Carolina, and when shooting there ended I flew back to Los Angeles. Upon arrival I headed from LAX straight to South Central to cop rock, then home to get high with Denise.

I stayed in the garage until my paycheck from the film cleared. Then I said goodbye to Denise and moved from her place out in the Valley to a cool one-bedroom in a West Hollywood apartment complex.

Margaret Avery, Quincy Jones, Dad, Whoopi Goldberg, and me on the set of The Color Purple.

WITH SUCH GOOD NEIGHBORS

One of my new neighbors—let's call him Barry—was delighted to meet the son of the world-famous actor/comedian.

Barry was originally from Brooklyn and dropped out of law school when his cocaine dealership took off. After a dispute with his supplier he thought it best to relocate the business. A good move: the SoCal climate suited him better and the entertainment industry thrived on cocaine.

Barry kept a nice supply of high-grade powder on hand and was extremely generous with it.

In fact, it's been my good fortune in life to develop close friendships with folks who were generous in sharing their drugs. (Nudge-nudge wink-wink.)

Of course, I knew Barry befriended me only to get to my father, a notorious coke user.

(In one of his routines, Dad says he snorted cocaine for 15 years. "I musta snorted up Peru." And in *Blue Collar*, he claims, "I did so much coke, I embarrassed my cocaine dealer.")

One time, while I sat in Barry's apartment and happily snorted his most excellent product, he took out a syringe and shot up.

Needles weren't my thing. That first time I saw him do it, I looked away and tried not to gag.

But a few days later, I was curious enough to watch.

"Here's what you do," he said, and described the procedure as he performed it. "First, you mix the coke with a few drops of water in a spoon."

He lit a cigarette lighter and held the spoon over the flame.

"Then you heat the shit till it starts to bubble."

The shit started to bubble. It smelled like piss on burning rubber.

"Then you dip your syringe in there, like so, and draw in every drop."

When all the liquid was sucked into the syringe he smiled. "And now, Richard, I want you to lay back, relax, and enjoy this."

"*What?*"

"Yeah. Like they say in the commercial, 'This Bud's for you.'"

I stared at the syringe, terrified.

"A slight pinch is all you'll feel."

"A slight pinch?"

"I promise."

Okay, I could deal with a slight pinch.

I lay back on the couch. He tied off my arm with a length of rubber hose, just like in a doctor's office. Or like Frank Sinatra in *The Man with the Golden Arm.*

I closed my eyes.

He tapped my arm.

"Ooh, you got some good veins, Richard. Let's see. Eeny, meeny, miny, moe."

I barely felt the pinch.

And then....

And then....

And then....

Aaaaaaaahhhhhhh ....

LIKE FATHER LIKE SON

I was hooked.

One time I was so stoned I decided to call Dad and let him know.

When the housekeeper answered the phone I asked to speak to him.

She said, "One moment, Richard Junior."

Dad got on the phone. "Hey, Son."

(He always called me "Son," never "Richard" or, God forbid, "Junior.")

"Heyyy, Daaad," I said in that drawn out voice you get when you're super stoned.

"What's up?" he asked.

"I'm hiiii-iigh."

I waited for a response. I figured I'd get anger, cursing, yelling.

Instead, he was quiet for a long time. Such a long time that I started to wonder if he'd already hung up the phone.

"Dad?"

"It'll be okay." After a few seconds, he added, "Yeah, you'll be all right."

I was certain, at that moment, that he was just as stoned as me, and we were connected through the telephone wire, on some coked out cosmic plane.

And maybe that's why I called him, for that connection.

It took years before I came to accept that we shared so many aspects of our lives: Peoria, Grandma Marie, the whorehouse and whores, the absent parent, the abuse. . . .

And, of course, the drugs, the alcohol, and the rage.

DOWN

Besides Barry, I befriended another neighbor, Jeff, who lived across the hall from me.

Jeff was a White bodybuilder, a big blond muscular guy with whom I soon started having sex.

What was weird was Jeff and I didn't really like each other. Jeff, from a poor family in Arkansas, was a bit of a racist. I treated him like George Jefferson treated his neighbor Harry Bentley; Jeff would knock on my door at all hours of the day or night and, if I wasn't in the mood—or just wanted to mess with him—I'd shut the door in his face.

Meanwhile: coke-dealer Barry. It must have dawned on him that I was not going to broker a meeting with Dad. Thus, I was no longer welcome to stop by for free product.

I resumed my South-Central runs to score crack, a much easier run now that I was in town and not way out in the Valley.

The thing is, it's impossible to hold a job when you're a crack-addict. As *The Color Purple* money started to run out I realized I needed a cheaper high. Since, thanks to Barry, I no longer feared jabbing a needle into my arm, I started shooting meth. The same South-Central youngsters who supplied me with crack were happy to sell me crystal meth, and even threw in a free syringe with my first order.

Pretty soon I had no appetite and only ate food when I remembered to. I lost 35 pounds. My arms swelled up from repeated needle jabs.

At some point, broke and desperate for a fix, I showed up at the home of Margaret Avery, an actress who played Shug in *The Color Purple*. I'd become friendly with her in North Carolina. I knocked on her door. She opened.

"Hi, Margaret."

She looked me over: "Hello, Richard, how are you?"

"Great. Terrific. How are you?"

"I'm well. Thanks."

She didn't invite me in.

"Margaret," I said finally, "I'm having trouble finding a job. I wonder if you could loan me, like, uh, twenty bucks."

"No, Richard, I'm sorry, I can't help you."

"Oh. Okay, well. . . ."

I turned and shuffled off.

Years later she told me she felt terrible about refusing me the money, but she knew it was for drugs and didn't want to contribute to my addiction. She added that as soon as I left she got down on her knees and prayed for me.

In fact, I have no doubt that she saved my life.

Thank you, Margaret!

WITH SUCH GOOD FRIENDS

Since I could no longer afford a fix, I went cold turkey. It was an awful few days, but somehow I kicked.

I got in touch with Mitzi Shore, who owned the Comedy Store and had previously employed me there as a doorman. She rehired me.

I loved the Comedy Store. I got a chance to watch a lot of great comics, both up-and-comers and established stars testing out new material.

I met Sam Kinison, a brilliant young comedian who had moved to Los Angeles after performing at small clubs in Houston.

Before he turned to comedy Sam had been a second-generation fire-and-brimstone Pentecostal preacher. He hadn't been very successful at it, though that aggressive evangelical style, punctuated with yelps and howls, became a distinctive trademark of his act in which he often poked hilarious fun at his former career.

Once we discovered we were both from Peoria we became close friends.

Sam, nine years my senior, took me under his wing, which meant nightly partying with his rowdy gang of Texas Outlaw Comics and the many rock stars in his orbit.

When you're determined to stay drug-free it's easy to refuse that first bump. When everybody in the room is snorting up lines, by the time you're offered a straw for the third time, you're like *Oh well, what the fuck.*

I relapsed.

Every night there were mountains of very pure cocaine, gallons of Jack Daniels, and, in the wee hours, valium, though some of Sam's friends opted for a snort of heroin to ease them down.

One time I was there when Sam bought some coke from his dealer. I wanted to buy a small amount as well, to share with him, but Sam, who had held the same lowly doorman job as me and knew how much salary I made, said, "Richard, put your money away, I got us covered."

Later that night, at Sam's house, the two of us flying high, he told me that he thought I was hot and wanted me to fuck him.

I was flummoxed.

I sat there, contemplating sex with Sam.

Hmmmm. . . .

Finally, I said, "Do you have any porn?"

"What the fuck, man! You need porn to fuck me?"

"No, it's me—my problem—I need to watch some porn before I can, you know, get it up."

We ventured into his bedroom and snorted a mountain of coke while watching a porn movie on his video-cassette player.

Eventually, we both got sexed up and everything went according to plan.

According to Sam's plan, at any rate.

A few more weeks of hanging out with him and his crowd and I knew it was time to make the call.

"Dad?"

"Hi, Son, how are you?"

No reply on my end, only silence. A long silence.

"Okay, don't worry, I got it."

During that next month in rehab there was the usual round of therapy sessions, physical activities, group meals, ping-pong—all the goodies I'd grown accustomed to from my stay in the psychiatric institute.

Some Comedy Store employees and a few of the comics came to visit and encourage me.

My first day out I returned to work at the Comedy Store, healthy and fresh, happy to be clean again.

First night on the job, Sam arrived.

"Welcome back, man," he said, and handed me a fifth of Jack Daniels and an eight-ball.

Ciao, Sam

After you've detoxed, there's nothing like that first shot of coke and booze.

Sam's place in the Hollywood Hills was party central. That sex thing I did with him was just a one-off, an experiment on his part, which was merciful news because I couldn't have done it again, even with all the cocaine and porn in the world.

Within a few weeks of cocaine- and Jack-filled nights, I knew it'd either be Rehab #3 or else I'd best get the hell out of Dodge.

I moved back to Peoria.

The next time I saw Sam he was performing in our hometown. He invited me on stage to sing "Wild Thing" with him. It was the perfect song for Sam.

(Historical note: When Sam hosted *Saturday Night Live* in 1986 he became only the second SNL host to air on a five-second delay, so his unbridled use of profanity could be bleeped out. The first such five-second-delay honoree? Of course, my dad.)

After the show, we hung out. Amazingly, neither of us were drinking or snorting. Still, we had a grand time catching up, reliving the "good old days," and laughing our asses off.

On April 10, my birthday, Sam's brother Bill called to tell me the horrible news. In LA, some drunk driver jumped the freeway divider and hit Sam's car head-on. Sam was killed.

I wept.

For days I asked myself *why?*

I just couldn't comprehend it. A man is on the path to recovery; he struggles with his demons and wins.

The only way I could accept his death was to conclude that it was God saying, "Nice work, Sam, you got yourself back together. Now I'm going to take you before you screw it up again."

From Drugs to Drag

Club Peoria was a gay club that held about 200 people, featured a nightly drag show, and smelled of stale beer. There was a dance floor with a mirrored disco ball and colored lights. During the shows the DJ played whatever songs the performers lip-synched to. Between shows there was dancing to stuff like "Sweet Dreams Are Made of This," "Hey, Mickey," and anything by Donna Summer or Grace Jones.

With my performing experience in Norfolk, I felt right at home getting up on stage.

I adopted a stage name: Rainy McKnight. Although I doubted that any member of my family would wander into the club, should that happen, there was little chance they'd recognize shy little Richie in my outrageous Rainy McKnight persona.

With all my moving from place to place, many of the gorgeous ensembles, wigs, and paraphernalia I'd acquired in New York were left behind or lost. To augment my act, I discreetly borrowed some of my mother's jewelry and a beaded or sequined dress or two.

My show evolved and, egged on by loyal fans, got weirder and weirder. Though I still performed the Jennifer Holliday *Dreamgirls* number, now, in black, I'd have the DJ declare with a cry, *She said she would never ever leave me!* Then the the stage lights would come on, I'd emerge from a coffin, and burst into "And I'm Telling You I'm Not Going."

I had learned at the Paradise Garage that you could diversify your music choices. I added some pop tunes to the typical drag repertoire of Broadway show tunes and disco hits. One pop number I performed was "Welcome to the Real World," a Mr. Mister song that featured Rainy McKnight dolled up as a Zombie Queen.

My most loyal fan was a dear handsome lad who showed up every night I performed and bought me drinks after the show.

His name was Jesse.

Rainy McKnight.

He was a White guy with light brown eyes, longish dark hair, and a slight overbite. When he laughed his tongue stuck out like a giggling lizard. Hilarious.

We started dating. We clicked and decided to move in together. We found a small house not far from the Club Peoria. Our home became

Diva Central. All the drag queens would come there to change into their stage gear, put on their make-up, offer each other bits of bitchy advice, and maybe smoke a joint and relax before a show.

Life was fabulous. I was in love with a guy who loved me back, and I was a rising star.

To top it off, Mom actually liked Jesse.

Partly, I think, because Jesse and I had our own place, so it wasn't like when I was with Larry and the tension that existed between her and me because "my condition" was "our little secret." And partly because Mom had gradually evolved her position on homosexuality—at least as it applied to her only son—and accepted the fact that I was unlikely to produce grandchildren for her.

Jesse would often visit Mom with two six-packs of Bud, her favorite beer. They'd sit around the kitchen, sometimes with Aunt Betty, who also liked him. If it was a nice warm day they'd hang out in the back yard and knock back a few brews while they shot the shit.

I felt so emboldened by Mom's new attitude that I invited her to a performance.

A SONG FOR MOM

Mom and Aunt Angie came to the Club Peoria to see my drag act. Neither of them had ever seen a drag show before.

Jesse helped me get into character: shoes, costume, wig, jewelry, makeup, everything had to be perfect and co-ordinate with the song we'd chosen: Grace Jones, "Slave to the Rhythm."

I've never had stage fright. Being up there in front of an audience, the center of attention, was always the best thing in life.

Yet on that night, as the DJ introduced Rainy McKnight, with Mom and Angie in the audience, I experienced the jitters.

But as soon as I stepped out on stage and was swept up by 200 cheering fans, I was on fire. Rainy's best performance ever. Tumultuous applause.

After the show I joined Mom, Jesse, and Aunt Angie at their table. Jesse high-fived me.

Angie gushed and raved about how terrific I was, how enjoyable the show, how proud she was of me, etc. etc.

My mother was silent.

"Mom, what did you think?"

"Those earrings."

Uh-oh. Her earrings. I forgot.

"Richie, I've been looking for them for *months*."

"I'm sorry."

"What about the black cocktail dress, with the sequins."

Fuck. I nodded, wanting to crawl into a hole and hide.

"Didn't I teach you the difference between borrowing and stealing?"

"When you borrow, you ask first."

"Exactly."

Angie interceded. "Come on, Pat, give the kid a break."

Mom glanced at Jesse, who was trying hard not to burst out laughing, his lizard-tongue darting in and out.

"I'll make sure everything is returned," he said.

Mom relented. "I loved the show. You were wonderful."
I floated on cloud ten, one cloud higher than nine.

JT

His birth name was Julius Taylor. He was born and raised in Memphis, Tennessee.

I don't remember when or how he and Mom first met, but they were together off and on for years. Like Harry—like my dad, in fact—he was a womanizer and abuser.

One time, Mom got a call from a friend that JT was at the Carver Community Center, very tight with another woman. Mom drove over in a rage and confronted him.

JT grabbed her by the throat and proceeded to choke her. Fortunately, there were other people there and they pulled him away.

When I heard about that incident I saw red. In a rage, I got into my car—a clunky old Subaru—shoved the two milk crates in place behind the driver's seat to keep it erect, and headed for Mom's house.

I parked in front.

Mom and JT must have patched things up again because they were out on the front porch with Granny, drinking beer and laughing.

Mom's brother, Uncle Gerald, was also there, but he wasn't laughing.

I stormed up to the porch, right into JT's face and said, "You ever lay a finger on my mother again, I will kill you."

"Get the fuck outta here, faggot."

"*What?*"

"You heard me! Get the fuck outta here, you fucking *faggot!*"

I turned and marched back to my car, popped the trunk, and grabbed the tire iron—a small one, for the Subaru's small tires.

When I turned around I saw that Uncle Gerald had popped the trunk of his own car, a big old Lincoln Mercury. I also saw that JT had emerged from the house with a big kitchen knife in his hand. He stepped off the porch and headed toward me.

Uncle Gerald handed me the Lincoln Mercury's tire iron, a much heftier tool than my own.

By now, Mom was screaming, "*JT, don't! JT!*" and Granny was crying "Oh Lord Jesus! Oh Lord Jesus!"

JT stopped two feet from me, his breath reeking of booze. He glared at me, trying to figure out whether to jab or slash.

I said, "Let me show you what a faggot can do."

He jabbed, I swung that tire iron down on his arm.

There was the *crack* of broken bone.

JT screamed and dropped the knife. Crying and moaning, he ran to his car, somehow got it started with his good hand, and sped off.

I like to believe that he never laid a finger on Mom again, but he sure as hell never again called me a faggot.

Bad News

It started with a phone call from Dee, one of the bartenders at Club Peoria.

I was home, getting diva-ready.

"Richard," she said, "there's some guy here asking for a photo of you."

"Cool. Give him one of the new publicity shots. I autographed a bunch."

"I don't know, I get a weird vibe from the dude. He doesn't seem like the kind of person who, you know, is turned on by a drag queen."

"Okay, thanks. See ya later."

By now, Rainy McKnight was not only the headline performer at Club Peoria, she was also the host, so I was used to flashbulbs going off while I was on stage. But that night, there was something different about the flashbulbs.

After the show Jesse met me in the dressing room and hustled me out the back door.

No use. The paparazzi were there, cameras flashing, and a guy who identified himself as a reporter for the *National Enquirer*. He demanded an interview.

Jesse and I ignored him, walking straight to my car.

The reporter followed us, saying, "Richard, do yourself a favor. Talk to to me. If you don't, we'll just print whatever we want."

I said, "Fuck off."

The next week, Dad was on the cover of the *Enquirer*, the *Star*, and the *Globe*, side-by-side with a glamorous performance photo of Rainy McKnight.

[Photo 26.]

I was horrified. Those three tabloids were prominently displayed at every check-out counter of every supermarket and drug store— in every gas station and newspaper stand—all across America.

My entire family would see RICHARD PRYOR'S SON IS A DRAG QUEEN.

There was hate mail. Mom received anonymous letters, like, "I thought you had two daughters, I didn't know you had three."

My sisters were mocked and harassed. I felt terrible for them and apologized profusely.

Dad was amused. Having me tagged as a drag queen was no big deal. Then too, with his many marriages, divorces, and crazy shenanigans, he was used to being tabloid fodder.

SCARLET A

After the Rainy McKnight *National Enquirer* brouhaha, things started to change with Jesse and me.

For one thing, I was unfaithful.

My sister Elanda just had a baby and I went to the hospital to see her. In the waiting room I started chatting with a real cute guy. He told me that he and his wife were from a small town near Peoria and his wife was in the hospital for lady-stuff.

We wound up going back to my place and doing the deed.

Yeah, while Jesse was at work and the guy's wife was in the hospital, we fucked.

A pair of dogs, right?

THE THING WITH JESSE

My afternoon delight with the guy whose wife was in the hospital was a sign, a signal that for Jesse and me, the frost was on the pumpkin.

Jesse' lizard-like smile, which I'd once found so adorable, now, when it did appear, just seemed . . . lizard-like.

We fought once. I don't remember what it was about, but it was just pushing and shoving, nothing like the Larry Woods beatdown in California.

Not that first time.

The shit hit the fan the day Craig called me.

Craig was an old pal from Peoria Heights High School. Back then, we called him Patricia. He was a real nellie, an effeminate very dark Black guy with big juicy lips, always flamboyant, except when he came to my mom's house. Then, he totally toned it down and became super-polite and respectful; he always called her Miss Pat. Maybe that's why we gave him the nickname Patricia.

Craig had just returned to Peoria after a stint in a Florida prison. He invited me out for drinks.

I called Jesse, told him where we were headed, and asked him to join us.

"Why?" he asked, "so I could listen to you two talk about your shitty childhood?"

"Come or don't come, whatever you want."

"I'm meeting Claudia."

Claudia was a co-worker friend of Jesse's, a loud-mouthed, stuck-up, opinionated White bitch.

Right, I didn't like her. Jesse knew that.

"Have fun," I said.

Craig and I were on our third round of gin-and-tonics when Jesse walked in with Claudia.

They joined us at our table and I made the introductions.

Jesse and Claudia both ordered frozen margaritas. We made small talk.

When the drinks arrived, Craig raised his glass.

Craig: "Well, cheers, y'all."

Claudia imitated him: "Well, cheers, y'all."

So did Jesse: "Well, cheers, y'all."

Me: "Cheers."

Craig was a sensitive soul. I hoped he hadn't picked up on their mockery.

In any case, he continued to catch me up on our friends from school who I'd lost touch with, particularly "Ike," whose mom and sister taught me how to shoplift.

Jesse fidgeted, obviously bored with talk about people he neither knew nor gave a shit about.

Claudia took it further: she yawned. I wanted to slap her.

Instead, I brought the conversation around to my alter-ego, Rainy McKnight, and the whole tabloid episode. Surprisingly, Craig knew all about it. His mom had sent him the *National Enquirer* clippings while he was in the pen.

At the mention of prison, Jesse and Claudia perked up.

"I hear," Claudia said, "there's a high rate of HIV and AIDS in the prison population."

Jesse added, "Especially among African-American males."

The comments surprised Craig, took him aback, like he couldn't figure out where these two White people were coming from.

Jesse ran with the ball. "You been tested?"

"No. You?"

"No. I'm very selective who I fuck."

Under normal circumstances, that would have been a compliment. In this instance, it was clearly a barb aimed at Craig.

"Jesse," I warned.

Claudia continued the attack. "I hear," she said, "there's this whole sexual hierarchy system in the slammer. Like, where a person is in the hierarchy determines whether he's a hitter or a catcher. You know, a top or a bottom."

Craig downed half his gin-and-tonic.

She wouldn't let it go. "So, Craigie, I'm kinda curious. If you don't mind my asking, were you a top or a bottom?"

"Claudia," I warned.

"*What?* An innocent question."

Craig glanced at his watch. "Aw shit, sorry, folks, gotta run, dinner wit' the Moms."

He stood and placed some cash on the table.

"Nice to meetcha, Jesse," he said. "Nice to meetcha, Claudia. Richard, as always."

As soon as he was gone Claudia turned to Jesse and said, "Nice to *meetcha*, Jesse."

Jesse laughed and responded in kind, "Nice to *meetcha*, Claudia."

Claudia looked at her wrist, which had no watch. "Aw shit, *sorry* folks, gotta run, dinner wit' the *Moms*."

She turned to me. "Richard, as always."

I stood and threw my drink in her face.

Before either of them could react I was out of there.

A wise move. I felt the rage coursing through me and knew I'd better chill out before I headed home.

I stopped into a gay bar where the bartenders knew me and drank three more gin-and-tonics. Two would have done the trick, but the third one was on the house, so, as a well-mannered customer, I had no choice.

When I finally staggered home I dug into my pocket for the keys. No keys. Fuck.

I rang the buzzer and waited. And rang again, a long one. And waited some more. It occurred to me that Jesse might not be home yet or already asleep. Then, the answering buzzer sounded.

I entered the apartment. He was fully dressed, so he'd just been fucking with me about the buzzer, to keep me waiting.

As soon as I was inside he went off. "How *dare* you toss a drink in Claudia's face!"

I wanted to punch him. Instead, I headed into the kitchen to get away. From earlier in the day, the ironing board was in there, with the iron still on it.

Jesse followed me. "Claudia is my *supervisor*, you fucking *loser*."

I whirled on him, rage in my eyes.

He must have sensed a fist heading his way. To prevent that, he grabbed the iron and smashed it in my face.

Blood.

Fuck.

I grabbed his wrist, the hand that held the iron, and twisted it hard.

He screamed and dropped the iron.

Then I punched him in the gut: three, four, five times. He tried to kick me in the balls, but I knew Jesse was the kind of person who would kick a guy in the balls. I anticipated that and turned aside.

We grappled, bouncing from the kitchen into the living room.

In the living room was a white wicker table with a glass top. We fell against it, shattering the glass.

Jesse grabbed a shard and jabbed at my eyes. He missed, but slashed my face just under my left eye.

I clutched his wrist, twisted the glass shard from his hand, grabbed it, and sliced it across his throat, cutting him from ear to ear.

Bleeding like a pig, he screamed and ran into the kitchen.

Even in my dazed state I knew he was going to come at me with a kitchen knife. I ran for the door but was so crazed I couldn't figure out how to unlock the damn lock.

Instead, I whirled around and ran to the balcony. Our apartment was on the second floor, only ten feet from the ground, but when I looked down it looked like the Grand Canyon.

I hesitated. Then, out of the corner of my eye—my unbloodied eye—I saw Jesse rush at me with, sure enough, a kitchen knife.

I vaulted over the railing, flew through the air, and hit the ground. Sprawled on hands and knees, I rolled over to see if Jesse was also going to jump and come after me.

No, he stood there on the balcony holding the knife, afraid to take the leap.

Sirens. Two police cars screeched to a halt.

Apparently a neighbor heard the ruckus and called 911.

As soon as the police saw the blood streaming down my face they phoned for an ambulance.

When they saw Jesse on the balcony, his throat slashed, blood gushing down his chest, they called for a second ambulance.

I was taken to Proctor Hospital, Jesse to Methodist.

Historical aside: the prior year, in September 1983, the Center for Disease Control published their first set of recommended precautions for healthcare workers and medical professionals to prevent AIDS transmissions.

Yeah. As soon as the medical professionals at Proctor and Methodist realized that Jesse and I were gay, none of them would touch us, while we lay there bleeding, until they ran HIV-AIDS tests.

We both tested negative.

Once that was settled we were admitted. As soon as I said the magic words—Richard Pryor Jr.—the top plastic surgeon in town was summoned. He performed a miracle on my face. You'd never notice the damage, there's not even a scar.

In the aftermath, an assistant district attorney from the Illinois DA's office interviewed both Jesse and me, separately, about pressing charges. Just in case, Dad retained a top criminal defense lawyer, but in the end, with both Jesse and I pointing accusatory fingers at each other, it came down to a he-said/he-said situation, with no way to prove who was culpable.

P.S. Jesse continued to visit Aunt Betty. Years after the bloodfest, years after I'd last seen him, years after I'd completely turned my life around, I visited Aunt Betty.

We sat in her parlor and drank beer.

She told me Jesse had stopped by a few months ago with something he asked her to give me.

She handed me a ring, a ring I'd given Jesse. He'd given me a matching one.

Engagement rings.

Yeah, we used to say we were engaged, though of course it was way before same-sex marriage became legal.

I picked up the ring and slipped it on.

CRITICAL CONDITION

In 1986 my father shot a film called *Critical Condition* on location in High Point, North Carolina.

In one of the few instances that Dad let me audition for a film he was in, I read for the small role of an ambulance driver. As it turned out, the casting director's first choice for the part was an upcoming actor named Wesley Snipes, who was then performing in an off-Broadway play in New York. Had the play received a great review and continued its run, I would have been the ambulance driver. But the play folded, Wesley got the role, and I ended up, yet again, a production assistant.

As is typical on a film shoot, the hours were long and the actual PA work consisted mostly of schlepping equipment and waiting: waiting for the hair and make-up folks to make the actors look good, waiting for the cinematographer to relight, waiting for the DP to reposition the camera, and waiting for the actors to run the same scene over and over and over until the director, producer, and stars all agreed on a take.

My first night in High Point I found a nice bar to unwind in after a long day on set.

Now, major film shoots in small towns like High Point are always a big deal for the locals. Plus, this was a Richard Pryor movie and I was Richard Pryor Jr. In no time I was chatted up at the bar by a friendly woman named Marlene and some of her pals. When the bar closed for the night we adjourned to Marlene's apartment.

And out came the cocaine.

My new friends and I partied all night.

Later, I swallowed some valium to come down, got a few hours of sleep, and dutifully reported in for production duties.

Being a creature of habit (no pun intended), I quickly fell into a routine: work, party, valium, sleep. Repeat.

Marlene was my coke connection. She delivered an order on a daily basis. Every lunch break I'd rush from craft service out to her car and score. The process made me laugh. It reminded me of third grade, when I had to miss lunch because Tammi was dismissed from her half day of kindergarten and I had to walk her to Karen's house.

Critical Condition filmed in the old abandoned Bacon Hospital.

I cleverly hid a vial of coke on every floor. Whatever set we shot in, I could quickly find my stash between takes and do a few bumps.

My routine proceeded like that for a few weeks until one night the drinking and partying was so intense that, even with valium, I couldn't fall asleep, couldn't get straight enough to show up for work.

Being a responsible member of the community, I called in sick.

The next day when I arrived for work an associate producer wanted to know why I had been a no-show.

"What? No, I called in and left a message."

The associate producer played the tape for me. No message.

I suddenly realized what happened. I'd been so coked up that I blurted out my entire message before I heard the beep, before the outgoing message was even finished.

Despite that, I continued to sneak bumps all day and party all night.

Finally, very late one night, or very early in the morning, I felt myself fall apart.

I sat in my hotel room. I'd done so much coke that I could only sit on the bed and grind my teeth. I couldn't bear to look at myself in the mirror. I hated what I saw. A fuck-up. An embarrassment to my father and myself.

I called Dad and—I couldn't help it—started sobbing on the phone.

"Dad, I need help! I can't go on!"

"Okay, Son, I'll take care of you. You'll be okay."

A few minutes later, Rashon Kahn, my father's assistant, came to my hotel room, packed me up, and drove me to the airport.

A half hour later we were on a chartered flight to Los Angeles, during which I cowered in my seat and babbled a non-stop stream of coke-fueled paranoia.

When we landed, Rashon drove me to Cedars Sinai Hospital.

I was checked in, and in an effort to bring me down, given a massive sedative, which worked way too well. It shut down my entire system.

Out-of-body, looking down at myself from the ceiling, I saw one nurse press my chest to stimulate my heart while another nurse yelled, "Richard, come on! Come on, Richard! Come on!"

My next memory was days later, sitting on the floor of my hospital bedroom, lighting a cigarette with my Zippo cigarette lighter.

I tried and tried, but couldn't get the damn cigarette lit.

Finally, I realized that I had no cigarette between my lips.

And no Zippo lighter in my hand.

WHO'S RUNNING THE ASYLUM?

I stayed in rehab for thirty days.

As my release date approached, a nurse asked about my aftercare program.

I told her I planned to return to Peoria as soon as possible, but until I left Los Angeles I'd continue to see the staff psychiatrist.

She gave me an odd look, which I noted at the time but had no idea what it was about.

The day after my release I called the hospital to set up an appointment with my shrink and was told he was no longer employed at the hospital. They referred me to out-patient care with a different psychiatrist.

While I had been in rehab I met a couple of patients that I grew friendly with and wanted to check in on. I walked down the hall past the pay telephone that was reserved for patients. There, talking on the pay phone was a man wearing an inmate gown and slippers.

I stopped dead in my tracks when I recognized him.

It was my former psychiatrist.

SAVING RICHARD

I was back in Peoria and living with Mom.

Purgatory.

I hadn't been to church in a while, though I still loved gospel music. On a whim, I went to a Saturday night concert by The Sounds of Deliverance at the Shrine Mosque.

Listening to those deeply spiritual songs, I felt the weight of the world lift an inch or two off my shoulders—enough to send me back to church the next day for Sunday services.

Everyone was friendly and welcoming. No one commented on my very gay appearance: permed hair, colorful shirt, flared pants, platform shoes, the whole shebang.

I went back the next Sunday, and the next.

The colorful shirts were replaced by pale-blue button-downs and striped ties; the flared pants with a navy-blue suit, de-mothballed and dry cleaned; and the platform shoes with a pair of black wing-tips.

Sundays rolled by. My hair grew in and I cut the perm.

There was a woman in the church I clicked with, Diane.

We clicked but didn't *click*.

What I mean is, when we started dating I was reluctant to mention my life as a gay man, my copious drug use, and my stints in rehab. On the flip side, she didn't tell me of her own drug use—heroin and crack—nor of the fact that she was still married.

The latter bit of information I discovered while reading the newspaper one morning and there, in the public notices section, saw the posting that the court had just granted her a divorce.

Rather than turn me off by the revelation, it opened a door to more honesty in our relationship. We dated for a couple of years. To keep up appearance with our church brethren, she had her place, I had mine.

(If you really must know, yes, we were fornicating.)

Eventually, everyone in church knew of our relationship. There was no judgment, no tsk-tsk, no Bible-thumping tirades about pre-marital sex. It was all very cool.

I moved into her apartment, where she lived with Marquita, her daughter from the previous marriage. The apartment was in a low-income housing complex; $40 a month rent for a large three bed-room with two bathrooms.

A year of happiness passed before the blessed event: Randise was born.

I was a father.

I called my mother with the news: "Mom, I know you're too young to be a grandmother, but guess what?"

"*Aaaaaaaa!*" This time it was a scream of delight.

I called Dad. As usual, a woman I didn't know answered the phone.

"Yes?"

"Hi, this is Richard Jr., can I speak to my father, please?"

"I see if he up."

She had some kind of accent, Spanish maybe.

A minute later: "Son? You okay?"

"Dad, congratulations! You're a grandpa!"

"*Yes!*"

"It's a boy. He's beautiful! We named him Randise. Randise Pry-or."

"Does he look like me?"

"Better looking!"

"Ha. Congratulations!"

"I love you."

"Love you too."

Diane and I decided to get married. There was no pressure from our church members or our pastor. We simply decided to do it. Decision made, I felt none of the panic I experienced prior to my almost-wedding to Sonia. This time, it felt like a natural extension of the life I'd been leading. I was comfortable with Diane, comfort-able with our little family, happy to be a dad.

We opted for a simple church service and scheduled it for three months after Randise's birth. Too late, we found out that Dad

Wedding day, 1992.

would be shooting a movie and wouldn't be able to attend. At least Mom would be there.

But then, two weeks before the big event, Mom was hospitalized with pneumonia.

When we visited her in the hospital we offered to postpone the wedding till she was better.

"No, Richie!" she said. "You go get married. I'll be there, God willing."

God was willing. Mom got released from the hospital on the very morning of our wedding, raced home to dress up, and made it to the church on time.

Dad was represented by his producer, David Banks.

Tammi was there, and Elanda, Marquita, of course, and aunts, uncles, cousins, and friends. Whatever embarrassment and anger I'd caused my family by the PRIOR SON DRAG QUEEN headline in the tabloids was forgotten.

It was a lovely ceremony.

Afterward we held a shindig at the Lakeview Center. It was a grand celebration. Delicious food, a terrific DJ, lots of dancing, toasts and speeches, hugs and kisses.

Regina Perkins sang a Patti LaBelle song, "When You've Been Blessed."

Entertainment Tonight mentioned the affair.

Neither Diane nor I were drinking alcohol, so our happy memories of that day are completely intact.

MS

Aunt Angie, Granny, Dad, and Mom on the set of Jo Jo Dancer.

In 1986 I was working at Domino's. I'd started off as a driver, delivering pizzas, and rose up to the elevated title of assistant manager. ("Son, whatever you do, do it all the way, the best you can.")

Dad had just completed work on *Jo Jo Dancer, Your Life is Calling.* Out of the blue he decided to drive his brand-new Ferrari Testarossa, with Deboragh, all the way from Los Angeles to Peoria.

They checked into the Juner's Castle Lodge, a German-themed hotel, and drove over to Domino's.

When they pulled into the parking lot I took a quick break and went out to greet them. In no time there was a crowd of fans gathered around the Ferrari, *ooh*-ing and *ahh*-ing, both for the car and for Dad.

I only had a few minutes, so we quickly made plans to meet for dinner.

As Dad left the parking lot, instead of a smooth exit down the driveway, he jounced off the curb.

I dismissed it as him being tired from the 2,000 mile trip.

But later, during dinner, when Dad excused himself to use the restroom, Deboragh confided that she was worried about his eyesight. On the cross-country drive, at night, he'd complained that his vision went in and out.

"Maybe he just needs a stronger eyeglass prescription," I offered.

"Maybe. As soon as we get back to LA, I'll set up an appointment."

Dinner was not a lot of fun.

Though Dad regaled us with amusing anecdotes about the cross-country drive, the humor was somewhat lost on my concern about his vision.

His frequent trips to the men's room meant he was tooting blow. Sure enough, before the entrée arrived, he offered me his vial of powder.

I didn't want to get into the fact that I was "clean," so I just demurred, "Oh, wow, Dad, thanks, I'd love to but I gotta be at work early tomorrow, like, six o'clock."

Deboragh raised an eyebrow at that and sipped her glass of chardonnay. She correctly surmised that never in the history of Domino's pizza had a customer ordered a pie delivered at six a.m.

They stuck around Peoria for a couple of days, then drove back to Los Angeles.

As soon as they got back Deboragh, scheduled an eye-doctor appointment.

Then another one.

Then a specialist for x-rays and blood work. Follow-ups. Another second opinion. An MRI. A third opinion.

It culminated in a phone call from her.

"Richard, I'm sorry to be the bearer of bad news. Your father has MS."

"What?"

"Multiple sclerosis."

Shock. Total shock.

"Richard?"

I stammered into the phone, "How long ... how long before ... ?"

"Every case is different. It depends on the individual how quickly the disease progresses. It could be months or years."

As she carefully explained the results of Dad's many medical tests, I began to sob uncontrollably.

Then Dad got on the line. "It's okay, Son, I'm gonna be fine. Don't listen to those asshole doctors. 'Ooh, he's got a compromised immune system.' What the hell is a compromised immune system!? You know me, I grew up in a fucking whorehouse. My mama was a whore and my daddy was a bruiser. You know what that makes me?"

Through my tears, I answered, "A ... a mean ... mother-fucker?"

"You said it, *a mean mother-fucker*. I ain't about to roll over for some bullshit fucked-up medical fuckin' *opinion*. Not without a fight. You dig?"

"Yeah. But, Dad?"

"Huh."

"Please don't die."

JENNIFER TO THE RESCUE

Jennifer Lee's 1991 marriage to Dad had lasted exactly fourteen days. After he divorced her she returned to New York, never to darken Dad's door again.

Until she heard that he'd been diagnosed with multiple sclerosis and was in pretty bad shape. Then, the self-described "tarnished angel" flew in and proceeded to bamboozle my father into a second wedding.

Rain told me that when she congratulated Dad on his marriage he just looked at her, puzzled.

"Your marriage to Jennifer," she said.

Dad's eyes went wide: *"Noooooo!"* he wailed.

BURN, BABY, BURN

It was January in Peoria. A foot of snow on the ground, icy roads, bitter cold.

We lived in a nice old house on North Street: Diane, her daughter Marquita, Marquita's four-year-old son Antwaun, my son Randise, and me.

Diane, Randise, and me.

Because I had to get up early to go to work I often slept in a bunk bed with Randise, me in the top bunk, him in the bottom.

At around two a.m., Marquita, who slept up in the attic space with Antwaun, woke me. "Dad, I think something's burning."

I sat up and sniffed the air. Yeah, something was definitely burning.

For dinner, I had cooked steak and baked potatoes. Did I leave a potato in the oven, with the gas burning?

I turned on a light. Smoke filled the room.

"*Shit!*"

I jumped down from the upper bunk. "*Randise, wake up!*"

I ordered Marquita: "Wake your mom! Call the fire department Everybody outside!"

Barefoot, in my boxers and t-shirt, I ran down the basement stairs to see what was going on.

Oh my God!

A fucking inferno!

Sheets of flame shot out from a crack in the furnace, the entire ceiling a blanket of fire. Right then, a burning beam fell and missed me by inches.

I raced back up the stairs, dodging cinders, and out the back door.

Diane, Marquita, and Randise were there, wrapped in blankets.

"Where's Antwaun?" I asked.

"*Oh God!*" Marquita started to run back to the house, but I grabbed her.

"*Stay here!*"

I ran to the house and threw open the kitchen door.

A deluge of smoke hit me, impossible to enter.

Sirens. Fire engines. Firemen jumped out and started to unspool a hose.

I ran up to one of them and pointed at the house. "*My grandson is in there!*"

He ran for the house, but with all the smoke, even he couldn't get in.

By now, a police car and an ambulance had arrived.

The firemen hooked up a huge fan to the kitchen door to draw the smoke out, then one of them ran inside. A minute later he came back out with Antwaun cradled in his arms.

Apparently, my grandson woke up and crawled down the stairs. He made it as far as the kitchen before the smoke overcame him and he passed out. That's where the fireman found him, on the kitchen floor.

Marquita ran for Antwaun, but the fireman who held him said, "He's not breathing," and handed the child to an EMT.

The EMT carried him into the ambulance and put an oxygen mask on him. Marquita and Diane, clutching Randise, got in there with them and the ambulance raced away.

One of the cops took a look at me. I was still barefoot, standing in a foot of snow and shivering in my boxer shorts on this freezing January night.

He said, "Sir, I think you better sit in the car for a while. Warm up."

I sat in the back seat of the cop car and they blasted the heat. As soon as it hit me, I started to scream. My feet were on fire, not from any burns I might have suffered, but from the ice and snow.

I had severe frostbite.

The police drove me to the same hospital Antwaun was in. He recovered right away, I was in a few days longer.

JENNIFER'S GENEROSITY

While I was in the hospital, Dad called. He opened with the standard parental question.

"You okay, Son?"

"Yeah, just real bad frostbite."

"What a pair we are. I set myself on fire, you freeze."

I laughed.

But then, "We lost everything, Dad."

"The house."

"Gone. All our stuff, clothing, everything."

"Shit."

"Even—remember that silver dollar you gave me at Grandma Ann's funeral?"

"You were six years old. You been carrying that mother-fuckin' coin around ever since? In the Navy and shit?"

"Yeah."

"Okay, don't worry. I'll have Jennifer get on the case."

For the next week or so, while Jennifer was "on the case," we stayed at a small outbuilding on the church's property.

Jennifer called. "Your father has a house for you," she said.

That house, in Bartonville, a town in Peoria County, was the one Dad bought years ago for Grandma Marie. After she died, Uncle Dicky lived there with his wife, Aunt Dee. After Uncle Dicky died, Dee stayed on and brought in some of her relatives.

When Aunt Dee got too old to take care of herself and moved into a nursing home, more of her family members took up residence in the house. None of them were Pryors.

Unbeknownst to me, Jennifer ordered Dee's entire family to vacate the premises. Had she informed me that she was going to evict people, I would've said no, we'll find another place.

Too late. The house was now empty. Diane and I fixed it up— fresh paint and wallpaper, carpeting, furniture—and we moved in.

Jennifer called.

"As a show of good faith," she said, "could you pay, let's say $250 a month?"

"Sure, I don't have a problem with that. Can you put it in writing, though? You know, that the house belongs to Diane and me?"

"Richard! You have to trust people!"

"Just send me a paper that the house is ours and I'll have all the trust in the world."

"Okay, *fine.*"

She never sent any document, so I never paid the $250 a month.

One morning, the county sheriff arrived with a court order that said we had to vacate within 48 hours.

Yeah, Jennifer had us evicted from the house Dad gave me.

LIFE GOES ON

Over the next couple of years, Dad and I spoke on the phone a lot. "I'm fine," he always insisted.

To prove his point, he flew Randise and me out to Los Angeles for a couple of weeks to demonstrate how strong and vibrant he was.

We scooted around town in the Testarossa. We had fabulous dinners at expensive restaurants. We went to a bunch of movies.

At a matinee for some film, I don't remember which, he bit into a candy bar, chewed, swallowed, and started choking. Couldn't catch his breath. I pounded his back until the bit of candy coughed up.

He saw the expression on my face.

Dad with the kids: Back row, Elizabeth, Rain, and me. Front row, Franklin Mason (Dad and Geraldine Mason's son), Dad, Randise, and Steven and Kelsey (Dad and Flynn's kids).

"Son, relax. I'm fine. Mother-fuckin' Almond Joy went down the wrong fuckin' tube."

While I was out there, Flynn—Flynn Belaine, Dad's wife #5 and #6— arranged for a professional photo shoot, featuring Dad and whatever children were available, plus his grandson, Randise.

When the prints came back, Flynn selected some smaller photos to be framed and placed them in the long hallway that led to Dad's bedroom. Those photos would be mixed in with other pictures of Dad's close friends and family members.

Inside his bedroom, on the wall across from his bed, Flynn hung a huge framed blow-up of Dad with the kids and the grandkid so he could see it first thing when he woke up and last thing before he fell asleep.

BYE-BYE HARRY

Remember him? Elanda's dad, who used to bang my mother's head against the wall?

Well, after Mom nearly stabbed him to death, Harry relocated 160 miles south to Alton, Illinois.

He remarried. The marriage didn't last long, but he and the ex stayed in touch. One summer day in 1995 when she hadn't heard from him in a while, she went to the house and found him lying on the couch.

Dead. A heart attack.

In a show of support for Elanda, I attended the funeral with her.

The mortician who did Harry's body screwed up. Harry's eyes weren't fully closed. It was creepy to see him stare at you through half-open eyes.

Elanda and I stood at the gravesite and watched the coffin lowered into the ground.

At least one of us had mixed feelings.

Seeing Red

In some ways, my wife reminded me of my mother; she was opinionated and spoke her mind, and when she embarked on a course, she stuck with it.

They were traits I admired—until speaking her mind meant constant criticism of me, and staying the course became bull-headed stubbornness.

Diane wanted to buy a new car.

"We can't afford another car now."

"Ask your father to buy us one."

"I'm a grown-up. I'm not gonna ask my father to buy me a car."

"What's the big deal? He's rich."

I said nothing.

"Why do you think I married you, anyway?"

I clenched my teeth.

That conversation repeated itself, with slight variations, almost daily for a week. My resentment silently built with each repetition.

Finally, of course, she just went and bought a new car, a bright red Ford fucking Prism.

I saw that car parked in the driveway and snapped.

I tore into the house.

Diane was in her favorite chair, one of those recliners with the foot rest that comes up when you lay back. She was laid back, feet up, reading a magazine.

Without a word, I reached down, grabbed the footrest in both hands, and yanked it up. The chair flipped backward, sending her flying.

Then I stormed out of the house.

At another time in my life, I'd have stopped at the first bar I came to and knocked back a few gin-and-tonics. This time, I remembered that our church had weekday services. I headed in that direction.

As I crossed the street to the church I glanced down the block and saw a bright red Ford Prism racing at me. I froze, terrified. At the last possible instant, I jumped out of the way.

Diane's new car whizzed by, a streak of red.

I ran inside the church. Sanctuary.

Service was in progress. A small afternoon congregation.

I stood in the rear of the nave for a minute, facing the pulpit, and took some deep breaths.

As soon as I felt calm enough to take a seat, Diane burst into the church brandishing a kitchen knife.

Escape was impossible, she was at the exit.

At the rear of the church was a gymnasium, separated from the nave by a moveable partition.

I ran for the gym.

A moment later she burst in and chased me, crazed, wielding the knife.

I ran back into the nave, down the aisle, screaming, "*She's trying to kill me! She's trying to kill me!*"

Yep, totally disrupted the service.

Diane didn't follow, she must have been too embarrassed. She ran outside.

I drew up whatever dignity I had left, found an empty seat, and sat down as if nothing out of the ordinary had occurred.

After the service the pastor's assistant took me into her office and asked me what the uproar was about. I explained the new car argument with Diane that had ended with the flipped-over chair.

"Richard, you shouldn't do things like that."

"I know. I just get so mad at her sometimes, so mad I can't hold it in."

"Well, next time, before you fly into a rage, try to contain yourself long enough to come here to discuss it."

"Okay. I will. Promise."

Feeling much calmer, I left the church and headed home.

As I crossed the street to our house, that bright red Prism came careening down the street at me again. This time, I was ready. Way before she got close, I ducked behind a tree.

FINITO AND BEYOND

I had to escape our marriage, but the thought of broaching the topic of divorce with Diane filled me with dread.

So I chose the chicken-shit option.

A year before the Ford Prism incident, under Diane's constant nagging, I had quit my job at Domino's and gotten a position at a company called AFNI, which did customer service for telephone companies like GTE and Sprint. In fact, I'd worked my way up to supervisor.

One day they posted a job position for a branch in Opelika, Alabama, where ever the hell *that* was.

I applied and got the job.

By this time Diane had become an evangelist minister. As such, she travelled around the country on speaking engagements. Shortly after I was offered the Alabama job Diane packed a bag for one such engagement in Florida. She would take Marquita along, as she often did.

Minutes before the two of them were to leave I told Marquita that I wouldn't be here when she and her mom returned.

As soon as they left for the airport I threw all my clothing into my car and hit the road.

Naturally, Marquita never mentioned my departure to Diane. When they returned, Diane flipped out. She went to AFNI and demanded to know where I was.

They told her I wasn't there any more, but would not provide her with any other information.

Unable to confront the fact that I'd simply walked out on her, she told people that she'd come home early from her speaking engagement, caught me in bed with a man, and kicked me out.

Regardless, I sent money to her every week, child support for Randise. But it was eight months after I left before I finally had the balls to call her up and talk. I apologized for running out on her like that, and told her where I was living and working.

I asked how she and Randise were. She said they were both fine and thanked me for the child support money.

She told me she had accepted a position at a church in New York City and would soon be moving there with the kids.

There was a brief pause, and then I said I was sorry I flipped her recliner chair over.

She said she was sorry she tried to run me down.

As soon as we made our apologies we both burst out laughing. The whole incident seemed so long ago, like it happened to two different people.

Two very silly, very ridiculous people.

Alabama

As soon as I settled into an apartment in Auburn, near my job in Opelika, my mind went, *Oh my God, I'm free!*

During my years of clean living with Diane, toeing the straight-and-narrow, a new crop of drugs had come on the market: ecstasy, special k, and ketamine.

I went crazy. Party-party-party. Pretty soon I was shooting that special k. Oh my, what a high!

BOBBY

That job in Opelika, that environment in Auburn—the whole crazy *Oh my God, I'm free!* thing—lasted less than a year. Then reality kicked in and I remembered how that story ends.

I asked my sister Elanda if I could stay with her. She had a small house but knew that while I was there I'd clear out her cabinets and reorganize them, put all her canned goods in alphabetical order. She happily invited me.

I quit my job, bid my farewells, and moved back to Peoria.

It was nice to see family and old friends again.

Soon, that stifled feeling crept in.

A cousin of mine told me that Qwest, another phone company, was hiring for a position in Des Moines, Iowa. I applied, got the job, and happily relocated.

The company found me a nice apartment.

At Qwest, I developed a crush on a co-worker, Mr. Robert Boucher. The crush was mutual, and Bobby moved in with me.

I thought we were in love, but soon I experienced the same old unease and suspicions I felt with Larry.

Sure enough, one evening I was walking home and heard a Grace Jones song spill out of a bar. I peeked inside, and there was Bobby lip-locked with some guy.

I restrained myself, held it in, and continued to our apartment.

When he got home I broached the subject of the guy he was making out with in the bar.

"Fuck you, Richard, I don't give a shit about your bourgeois morality! I don't love you! *I never loved you!*"

Of course, I snapped. It was a Larry-level snap though, somewhere between a Diane flip-the-chair-over snap and a Jesse bloodletting snap. Yes, I wanted to murder him, but in a supreme exercise of maturity and self-control I just punched him once, threw a glass against the wall, and broke a chair. Nothing serious.

I was proud of myself. I finally understood that if you reach a stage in your relationship where you want to murder your partner, it's best to just end it.

I ended it with Bobby.

A few months later we ran into each other. He apologized for cheating on me.

I apologized for my punching him.

We hugged.

Soon after that I learned that Bobby had passed. He got what we called the Gift, as in The Gift that Keeps on Giving.

AIDS.

I'm sorry, Bobby.

RYAN

This guy named Ryan also worked for Qwest.

Ryan was totally straight, totally hetero, kinda macho even.

To save on rent, we decided to move in together. We found a place in Altoona, Iowa, a suburb of Des Moines. We explored Altoona and discovered a bar with karaoke nights. Another reason Ryan and I became such good friends: he loved karaoke as much as I did.

I told the woman who ran the karaoke machine that I wanted to sing "Slave to the System." She said no, I should do "Sittin' on the Dock of the Bay" and Ryan should pick a Billy Joel song.

Apparently, that was typical behavior for the Nazi karaoke lady.

We left and found another bar called Old Town Tap. It was on a side street and I was apprehensive about going in. You know, a White dude and a Black dude in Altoona, Iowa.

Ryan assured me it would be fine. We went in and, sure enough, everyone was really nice and friendly. There was a pool table. We had a couple of drinks, shot some pool, and met the owner and his wife, Jay and Kylie. Jay told us that tomorrow was karaoke night, if we were interested.

Of course we were interested!

We went back the next night and, with all due modesty, tore the place up. Although Ryan may have had a better voice than me, my Rainy McKnight stage presence knocked 'em dead.

At the end of the evening Jay told us karaoke was very popular in Altoona (who knew!) and he wanted to expand it except that neither he nor his wife had the time to run the bar *and* three nights a week of karaoke. He asked if Ryan and I would like the job.

No pay, but all the Jack Daniels we could drink.

Yeah! My kind of paycheck.

MORE JENNIFER

Not long ago social media was all abuzz about a Quincy Jones interview in which Quincy said, about the great actor Marlon Brando, "He'd fuck anything. Anything! He'd fuck a mailbox. James Baldwin. Richard Pryor. Marvin Gaye."

(Okay, Quincy Jones is a genius, but he's like 200 years old and probably losing his grip, so let's forgive him for comparing sex with three of the greatest Black talents of his generation—James Baldwin, Marvin Gaye, and my father—to fucking a mailbox.)

Then I read on TMZ that "Richard Pryor's Widow" confirmed what Quincy Jones said, that my father had sex with Marlon Brando, and I wondered why Jennifer would step into that shit.

Jennifer also referred to the Pryor children as mistakes, conceived because Dad was just too lazy to put on a condom.

I reflected on Jennifer Lee.

It's hard to put my finger on the circumstances surrounding her rise to prominence in Dad's life. It seems to me that one minute she was an employee; a minute later they were dating; two minutes later she moved in; three minutes later they were married. (Of course, four minutes later they were divorced.)

Grandma Marie and Uncle Dicky couldn't stand her. Marie referred to her as "that phony White bitch."

For my part, I had no feelings about Jennifer one way or the other. But I was young and impressionable. I soon soaked up Grandma Marie's and Uncle Dicky's negative feelings toward her.

And Jennifer definitely had an attitude, particularly once she'd moved into the house, an attitude that proclaimed *I'm taking over now, I'm in charge.*

Family legend has it that Grandma Marie paid Dad's Creole cook to beat Jennifer up to teach her a lesson in respect.

See, Dad had this Creole woman who was his cook when he shot *The Toy* in Louisiana. He liked her cooking so much he hired her to come work for him in Los Angeles.

Grandma Marie and this cook hit it off; they both had a habit of smoking a cigarette while they cooked. Countless times I'd watch Marie as she stood over the stove and stirred a pot of stew with a Pall Mall cigarette clenched between her lips. I'd stare mesmerized as that cigarette burned down into ash and wonder why the ash, no matter how long it got, never fell into the pot of stew.

Whenever Grandma Marie was asked if she really hired the cook to beat up Jennifer, Marie always just laughed, like the very idea was preposterous, hilarious.

Yet shortly after the alleged incident, that Creole cook was gone.

For Jennifer's part, years later she often told the heart-wrenching tale of when she sat at Grandma Marie's bedside, after Marie had suffered a major stroke. According to Jenifer, Marie grabbed Jennifer's hand and said, "Promise me, after I'm gone, you'll take care of my darling Richard."

Two glitches in that story. One, Grandma Marie always called dad "Richie," never "Richard"—unless he'd fucked up and she sent him out to get a switch so she could give him a whupping.

Two, after Marie's stroke in 1978, she couldn't speak coherently, not a word; only gibberish came out of her mouth, never anything anyone could understand.

GRANDMA MARIE

In December 1978, Marie Carter Pryor Bryant died in Peoria's Methodist Medical Center. She was 79 years old.

Her funeral was held at the Church of God in Christ, in Decatur, Illinois, where she was originally from.

The entire family was present: Uncle Dicky, Aunt Maxine, my mom, Cousin Denise, Aunt Betty, and a slew of aunts, uncles, cousins, friends, and relatives. Folks came from far and wide.

Dad was distraught, broken, inconsolable.

Grandma Marie's Funeral. On the left, Uncle Dickie, me, Rain and Elizabeth. Dad is a pall bearer.

A FAVOR FOR MY FATHER

One summer day, after Jennifer had moved in with Dad but before they were married, she was out getting her nails done. This was back when I was in high school and spending my summers in the guest house.

Dad knocked on the door. When I opened he grabbed me by the arm and led me back to the main house. On the way, he hurriedly explained that there was a girl in his bedroom, coked out and refusing to leave. He was scared that if Jennifer found the girl in his bed there'd be hell to pay. He wanted me to go in there and have sex with her.

I held back, hesitant.

"Son, please, you don't have to fuck her, just get naked and lie on the bed with the bitch. If Jennifer comes home, I'll get all up in your face, 'Nigga, why can't you bring your bitches to the guest house?' But that's just between you and me. Okay?"

It's wasn't okay. The idea of getting naked with a woman my father had just fucked seemed . . . well . . . *weird*.

"Oh, hey," he said, "there's blow on top of the bureau. Help yourself."

Ah, blow. The magic word.

I entered Dad's bedroom. The door closed behind me.

Lying on the bed, naked, was one of the most beautiful women I'd ever seen. She showed no reaction to me being there instead of my father. Either he'd warned her about the switch or she was just too coked out to give a shit.

I went to the bureau. There was a mirror, a razor blade, a straw, and a large mound of coke.

I laid out two lines and snorted one.

Damn, Dad had some very fine shit.

I snorted the other line.

From the bed I heard, "*Me, too!*"

I carried the mirror and paraphernalia over to the girl and lay down with her.

She did a couple of lines with the straw, then sprinkled some powder on her left breast.

I snorted it up. No straw, just nostril to tit.

After that, there was blow on right tit, blow in belly button, blow on dick—a night of coke-fueled sex.

Weeks later, I was thumbing through an issue of *Hustler* magazine; the girl in Dad's bedroom was the centerfold.

LEMON FUCKING CHICKEN

As soon as Jennifer and Dad got married that first time—the marriage that lasted 14 days—she traipsed to the guest house and pounded on the door. I opened it. She brandished her left hand an inch from of my face so I could get a good close-up of her ring finger.

She grinned in triumph.

"Congratulations," I said, and shut the door.

Jennifer was a terrible cook. One evening she made lemon chicken from some recipe she found in a magazine. It tasted like that poor chicken had perished in a pool of sulfuric acid, but I didn't want to hurt her feelings, so I ate every morsel of that foul fowl, and constantly complimented her on the tasty bird.

Thereafter, every time I was invited for dinner I'd hear, "Richard, I made your favorite dish—lemon chicken!"

ANOTHER DEATH IN THE FAMILY

Meanwhile, back in Altoona, Iowa, besides my job at Qwest, I got promoted at The Old Towne Tap from running karaoke with Ryan three nights a week to becoming a part-time bartender.

One morning I got a call from my mom that she was having trouble breathing and was worried she might have bronchitis.

I called in sick to Qwest, told Jay I'd be gone for a couple of days, and made the four-hour drive from Altoona to Peoria.

As soon I arrived I took her to the hospital.

The ER doctor examined her, took some X-rays, and delivered the news.

"I'm sorry, Mrs. Price, you have a tumor on your left lung. We'll need to follow up and see if it's benign or malignant."

The follow-up confirmed the worst possible diagnosis: Mom had lung cancer.

They would begin chemo and drugs the following week, but the prognosis was not good. Six months at most.

My mother was a deeply religious person and took it as a matter of course that sooner or later she would be with God. If it was sooner rather than later, well, that was God's will and she was in acceptance.

I wasn't in acceptance. No, after the initial shock wore off I was devastated.

I told her I'd quit my job and move back to Peoria to be with her, to take care of her.

"That's very sweet, Richie, but I can't let you do that. Go back to Altoona, back to your job. Live your own life. Come visit when you can and don't worry about me."

I don't know how I drove home, four hours, crying the whole way.

I felt deep down that I would not survive without Mom in the world.

I knew what I had to do.

That night, at home in Altoona, I sat down at the kitchen table with a bottle of Jack Daniels, a pitcher of water, and my meds.

There was Ambien for sleeping and Wellbutrin for depression.

When Ryan came home he found me passed out at the table, head in arms.

He called my aunt.

"Angie, I think Richard swallowed a whole bunch of pills.

"Oh, God, get him to a hospital! *Right away!*"

On the drive to the hospital I fell asleep again.

Ryan yelled, "Richard! Wake up!

I didn't.

He pulled into a mini-mall and called 911.

"*I need an ambulance!*"

"Where are you, sir?"

He looked around.

"I'm in a McDonald's parking lot," he said, and gave the location.

By coincidence, an EMS team happened to be on a dinner break at that very same McDonald's, their ambulance parked on the other side of the lot.

They whipped around, loaded me into the vehicle, snapped an oxygen mask on my face, and we zoomed to the hospital.

I was unconscious for two days.

Ryan and Aunt Angie tried to keep my condition secret from Mom, but she kept asking, "Where's Richie?" and growing more and more worried. Finally, Angie broke it to her, that I was in the hospital, but not to worry, I'd "accidentally" swallowed too many sleeping pills, I'd be fine soon enough.

After my release I took off from work once a week and drove to Peoria to visit. Several times Ryan came with me.

Mom liked him, particularly after he'd taken care of me during my attempted suicide. She once told him, "Ryan, please watch out for Richie when I'm gone."

JT Sends Regards

At some point after JT called me a faggot and I broke his arm with a tire iron, he and Mom split up.

He got into crack, smoking it and dealing it.

He got busted and sent to prison.

When Mom heard, she started writing to him in prison.

He responded, describing the hardships of prison life.

She sent him money on a regular basis so he could buy cigarettes and whatever amenities were obtainable behind bars to make life easier.

A year or so after Mom's cancer diagnosis, JT was paroled. When Mom heard the news her spirits lifted. She so looked forward to seeing him again.

JT never called, never visited. Nothing.

It broke her heart.

I wished I'd fractured his skull with that tire iron.

LAST WISHES

Mom was much more concerned about the possibility of her hair falling out from the chemo than she was about dying. She constantly wished, hoped, and prayed that she wouldn't go bald and look sick.

She never did lose her hair. And when friends and family saw her, they were always astonished by how healthy she appeared.

On one of my visits she asked what was going on with my father.

"Every time I call him, some woman answers and says Richard can't come to the phone. I called again yesterday, and a different woman got on the phone and said he doesn't want to talk to me."

"Jennifer Lee. His wife."

"I thought he divorced her."

"They remarried, and she got Dad to assign her power of attorney. She runs his life, who he can see, who he can't see, who he can talk to, who he can't talk to."

She thought about that for a minute. Mom and Dad didn't have a bad relationship, she just wanted to talk to him, that's all.

"Richie, what about you? Maybe if you call him and he gets on the phone, you can hand me the receiver and—"

—I shook my head, no.

"I'm sorry, Mom. I haven't seen or spoken to Dad in three years."

THREE YEARS AGO

I was training for a job at a telephone company, GTE, in Victorville, California, about an hour and a half drive northeast of Los Angeles. One day I drove down to visit.

A servant let me into the house and I walked down the long hall that led to his bedroom.

The hall was stripped of every single photo, both the family and friends' photos and the ones from the photo session Flynn had set up. All that remained were tiny holes where the picture-frame hooks had been.

Inside the bedroom, the blow-up of Dad with the kids was also gone.

Dad was propped up in bed.

He looked happy to see me.

The servant stood discretely in the corner, in case we needed anything.

I sat by his bed. Conversation was difficult for him, I did most of the talking. I caught him up on what I was doing, told him some family news and gossip, cracked a couple of lame jokes.

At some point I asked him, "Remember that house you gave me, after the fire?"

He nodded.

"Jennifer kicked us out," I said, "and sold it."

He was surprised, confused, upset.

I immediately felt sorry that I'd mentioned it and quickly changed the subject. I talked about Randise and how well he was doing in school.

After a while, I could tell he was getting tired.

I kissed him goodbye and told him I loved him.

The servant escorted me out of the bedroom and closed the door.

Jennifer was waiting in the hallway.

I asked her about the photos.

"I'm having the place painted," she said. "And while the pictures are down, I'll have them reframed. Those old frames are tacky."

A month or two later I drove down to Los Angeles again to see Dad. On the way I stopped in at Flynn's to see if she'd like to join me.

She said she hadn't seen Dad in two years.

I was stunned, "How come?"

"Jennifer. She's cut his closest friends out of his life. Me included."

"That's crazy!"

"Richard. Be careful."

I drove the rest of the way to Dad's on edge.

I parked outside the gate, got out, and rang the bell.

A woman I'd never seen before, who I assumed was the house-keeper came out.

"Hi," I said, "I'm Richard Pryor Jr. I'd like to see my dad."

"One minute."

Instead of opening the gate, she went back inside. I waited. Five minutes later she returned.

"I'm sorry, Miss Jennifer say I can't let you in."

With that, she went inside and shut the door.

I was furious.

I called the police.

When the police arrived I explained the situation, that I was worried about my father.

They told me to ring the bell again. I did.

The same woman emerged, surprised to see the police there, but maintained that she couldn't let them in.

"I'm sorry, but—"

"—No," a cop said, "we have to check on him. Open the gate."

She glared at me, but opened the gate.

The cops went into the house while I waited.

Soon, they came back out.

"Yeah, your father wants to see you."

"Thank you, Officer."

I went inside.

I walked down the hall that led to the master bedroom. The hallway had indeed been painted, and the little holes where the photo-frame hooks were had been plastered over. But none of the previous photos were rehung.

Instead, the only photos on the walls were of Dad and Jennifer. Yeah.

I went into Dad's bedroom. The woman from the front gate followed me in, along with another woman and the servant who'd attended Dad when I last visited. I realized he must have reported my conversation with Dad, about Jennifer kicking us out of the house he gave me.

The three of them stood stiffly against the wall, like sentries on alert.

"Hello, Dad," I said.

He managed to eke out a "Son," his voice high-pitched and labored.

I sat on the bed, near him. I did all the talking.

The three sentries stood there the whole time, like a Southern California version of those guards outside Buckingham Palace in London, just watching and listening, poker-faced.

After a while, he was clearly drowsy.

I leaned close and whispered in his ear.

"I love you."

His lips tried to form an "I love you too" response, but not much came out.

I left.

The whole while I was there, Jennifer didn't appear.

I did not want to have to call the police every time I came to see my father, so I consulted a lawyer, who advised that I file for conservatorship.

"If we win," he said, "the court will appoint you as legal guardian to manage your father's financial affairs and daily life, due to his physical condition."

Since I was filing the papers, I had to name myself as the would-be conservator. In response, Jennifer filed a restraining order against me. It basically stated that I'd shown up at Dad's house unwanted and uninvited, harassed him, and terrified Jennifer and the servants.

The judge denied my motion for conservatorship and granted Jennifer the restraining order against me.

I would not see Dad again for six more years.

MOM

On one of my hospital visits Mom asked me to work on the program for her funeral. She made me promise to sing a song there.

The chemo and other drugs slowed the progress of the disease; the six months of life the doctor had predicted went blessedly on for eighteen months.

But inevitably there came a time when her condition required that she be moved from her house into a hospice situation.

Mom was terrified about spending her last days in a strange place surrounded by dying strangers, so we moved her into her mother's house, where Granny set up a hospital bed in the living room.

Mom at Granny's.

Granny, a confirmed hypochondriac who had "survived" lupus, diabetes, shingles, bird flu, and Ebola, to name a few of her fatal diseases, now insisted she had cancer. We figured it was Granny being Granny.

One night, I held Mom's hand and felt how icy cold it was, like her body was conserving energy, conserving heat by shutting down the blood-flow to her extremities.

With her eyes shut, she kept asking, "When's He gonna come for me? When's He gonna come?"

I called Aunt Angie and told her to get to Granny's as quickly as possible.

Angie arrived and held Mom's hand.

Mom asked again, "When's He gonna come for me? Huh? When?"

Angie gently squeezed her hand.

"Pat," she said, "do you see the angels?"

Mom's eyes fluttered open. She smiled, closed her eyes, and breathed her last.

My mother passed at 9:35 p.m., Friday, September fifth, 2003.

CLEANED OUT

The day after Mom's funeral, Granny's "cancer" took a turn for the worse.

To humor her, Aunt Angie and I drove her to the hospital. After tests and consultations with specialists, the diagnosis arrived. Granny was in the final stage of gastrointestinal cancer.

Four months after Mom died, Granny passed.

At her funeral we marveled at her courage, how she disregarded the terrible pain she went through long enough to take care of her daughter.

Another thought weighed heavily on us: the older generation had all passed. Grandma Marie, Grandma Ann, Grandpa Fox, Grandpa Buck—oh yeah, I forgot to mention Grandpa Buck's death. He had a fatal heart attack at age 57, while having sex with an 18-year-old girl. Dad joked that his father "came and went at the same time."

Now Mom and Granny, the two essential links that held the family together, were gone.

Granny and me.

A Personal Matter

Over the six years Jennifer legally prevented me from seeing Dad, she allowed my sisters to see him, one at a time, once a month each.

During the sixth year, my sister Elizabeth had an idea: she would give up one of her visits if Jennifer allowed me to see Dad instead.

Jennifer refused.

Elizabeth stuck with it. She emailed Jennifer that, with Dad's condition terribly deteriorated, there was no point in keeping me from taking one of Elizabeth's visitations, unless it was a personal matter.

Jennifer relented, but there were conditions.

One of the conditions was that Jennifer's friend Veronica be present for the meeting.

Seeing Dad after all that time was a terrible shock. He could barely raise his head and couldn't speak at all. Only his eyes revealed a spark of life, and then only occasionally.

I sat on the bed and held his hand.

At some point, I said, "Dad, do you remember my mother, Pat? Your first wife?"

After a moment, he blinked.

I continued. "She died. Two years ago."

His eyes filled with tears.

I told him I loved him and gave him a hug.

BAD NEWS

December 10, 2005.

I was still in Altoona, Iowa, living with Ryan, both of us working at QWEST while running the Old Towne Tap karaoke lounge three nights a week and tending bar part-time on the weekends. I was home when I got the call from Ryan.

"Richard, I . . . I have to tell you . . . Flynn just called."

I was surprised. "Flynn?"

"She couldn't reach you, so she called me to . . . give you the message."

"Uh-huh."

"I'm sorry. Your dad passed."

I was numb, silent.

"Richard, you alright?"

"Yeah."

"I'm sorry to tell you this over the phone instead of in person. I just wanted to let you know before you saw it on TV."

"I . . . I better . . . make some calls. Tell the family."

A minute after I hung up the phone rang again. It was Rain, and she just sobbed hysterically. There wasn't much we could say to each other, a few useless words of comfort.

Then the doorbell rang and it was Jan, a cocktail waitress from the Old Towne Tap. They had the TV on in the bar when CNN broke the news, and she came by the house to see how I was doing.

So I went back to the bar with her and sat there and watched the story repeat and repeat, all the ups and downs, the nooks and crannies of my father's life.

That's one thing that's really tough about being a child of a celebrity: a lot of things that are extremely personal suddenly aren't personal any more. My father's death was shared by the world and the world grieved, but for his children the grief was very different.

Our father was dead.

Final photo.

GOODBYE, DAD

Jennifer flew me out to Los Angeles for the funeral. She also flew Randise in from New York.

When my son and I arrived we went straight to Rain's house. We needed a place to stay and I knew we'd be welcome in her home. Besides, Elizabeth and my other siblings—Mason, Steven, Franklin, and Kelsey—were there, so we could cry on each others' shoulders, share our grief, and console one another.

Then Jennifer phoned. She screamed on the phone nonstop that we were only at Rain's house so we could conspire against her.

"I *know* you are! *All* of you, always *conspiring against me!*"

She didn't get that we had lost our father and needed each other's company now. No, it was all about Jennifer. It was always about Jennifer.

She demanded that Randise and I stay in the hotel with Flynn's kids, Steven, and Kelsey. I was too beaten down to argue.

She also informed us that there would be a closed coffin followed by cremation, so if we wanted to pay our final respects we should go to the mortuary.

Dad had never discussed cremation with any of us. In fact, it sounded like a horrible joke: Jennifer would complete the job Dad had once set out to do—immolation.

But Jennifer was in charge and there was nothing to be done except go to the mortuary to pay our respects.

When we got there, we were shocked.

Dad's body lay on a gurney-like table, his head propped up on a block. His face was terribly swollen. There was a sheet over his body, but you could tell it was also bloated.

We only stayed a few minutes. We said goodbye, told him how much we loved him and how much we'd miss him.

The Jennifer Lee Memorial

On the day of the funeral, a Hummer limousine arrived to take us to Forest Lawn.

A separate limo delivered Rain and Elizabeth.

When we arrived we entered the friends-and-family room. There were people I hadn't seen in ages. We hugged and traded condolences.

Inside the chapel, the Pryor family was ushered to seats on the right side, except for Rain and Elizabeth, who were seated on the left side, by themselves.

More of Jennifer's divide-and-conquer approach to dealing with us. I felt terrible for my sisters, it was a pathetic site.

I took a quick glance around the room.

The only friends of Dad's I recognized were Michael Epps, George Lopez, Mo'Nique—sitting in the back with Pauly Shore and his mother, Mitzi Shore—the one-and-only Ms. Diana Ross, and Argus Hamilton, a comic.

Where were the other people who mattered in my father's life, the friends and relatives who cared for him, admired him, loved him?

None of them had been invited. None were there.

George Lopez and Mike Epps spoke at the service. I can't remember a word they said.

Mo'Nique got some laughs when she quipped, "This is my kind of funeral—you can say *damn*, *shit*, and *fuck* without an issue."

The person who delivered the eulogy was a White German woman. I had no idea who she was, and she clearly knew nothing about Dad. She read the entire eulogy word-for-word from a printed text: a factual recounting of my father's seven wives, how he had married *this* woman and *that* woman and then this *other* woman and *that* other woman, until he finally met the *love of his life*.

Jennifer Lee.

Polite applause.

At the conclusion, Jennifer moved to the podium.

Before she could speak, Elizabeth yelled, "*You killed our father!*"

Jennifer said a few words and turned on the tears.

Afterward, we all rode together to a luncheon she had planned. It was only when we got there and were seated that I realized Elizabeth and Rain weren't there.

They weren't invited.

WELCOME TO NEW YORK!

After Dad's death I returned to Altoona and resumed my routine at QWEST and The Old Towne Tap.

But I felt unmoored, unsatisfied. *Is this what my life is about? Tending bar and cleaning the taps on weekends?*

I quit my jobs, said goodbye to Ryan, and moved back to Peoria.

I stayed with my sister Elanda again.

I hadn't formulated any plans yet when I got a phone call from someone in New York City, a gentleman named Marty Fisher.

Marty was organizing a festival at a New York comedy club, The Improv, at which they were going to dedicate one of the rooms to my father: The Richard Pryor Room. Would I come and be a part of it?

Of course!

Marty sent me a ticket and I flew to New York. He asked me to perform a stand-up routine for the festival. I explained to him that

Dad and I had a lot of things in common, but a talent for stand-up was not something we shared.

Instead, I sang a song, "His Eye is on the Sparrow."

The audience response blew me away: cheers, whistles, and applause that went on and on.

Afterward, people kept coming up to me to say how terrific I sounded. I was a little freaked because New Yorkers are known for speaking their mind, letting you know in two seconds if they think you suck. Apparently, I didn't suck.

New York, New York, it's a wonderful town!

We partied after the show. Neither Marty nor anyone in his office told me what time my return flight to Peoria was until six a.m., when one of his assistants "reminded" me that the flight out of LaGuardia was in twenty minutes. That wasn't going to happen.

For reasons unknown, a round-trip New York–Peoria ticket was cheaper than a one-way flight, so that's what they booked for me.

I arrived in Peoria, practically penniless, called my sister Rain, who sent me $300, and I turned right around and flew back to New York.

And never left.

Scuffling

I knew one or two people who would let me crash on their couch for a few days here and there.

I heard that this theater group, the Downeast Art Center on Thirteenth Street and Avenue A was auditioning performers for an event called The Cringe Festival, featuring plays so terrible they were brilliant.

I read for a woman named Melba LaRose. She offered me a part in a play called *The Best Little Crack House in Philly*. It was a musical and so over-the-top cringe-worthy that, well, one of the songs we sang had this lyric: "There's another dead baby on the dirty crack house floor."

Best Little Crack House in Philly.

Melba was wonderful and gracious to me. Once she learned that I didn't have an apartment and very little money she let me live in the theater.

At the end of every night, after the house emptied, I unfolded an Army cot and some blankets and slept on the stage. I had a little electric burner where I cooked food and made coffee, and I hung my clothes on a wardrobe rack.

The only downside was the rats. One or two would emerge every night and poke around. I'd wrap the blankets tight around me and whisper, "Not tonight, Mr. Rat, not tonight, please."

After the festival ended Melba allowed me to stay on. She also invited me to an event honoring this lawyer, Howard Blau. He and his girlfriend, Ann Kayman, also an attorney, were very involved with Broadway Cares, a non-profit for fighting HIV/AIDS.

At the afterparty, Howard asked me what I did. I told him I had recently arrived in the City to pursue an acting career.

He asked if I needed a day job.

"Yes."

"I have some temporary office work you could do, it pays $20 an hour."

Before I said "great," his girlfriend Ann said to him, "I have more work for Richard now than you do."

The next day I started as an office temp for Ann's business, the New York Grant Company. I'm still there today. We write grant proposals for commercial businesses. From office temp, I worked my way up to executive assistant: I interview prospective employees, solicit clients, and write up grant proposals which, if successful, pay me a commission.

(Oh, and Ann's boyfriend the lawyer?)

(He was convicted of stealing clients' escrow accounts, got disbarred and went to prison.)

Migraines

Recently I started getting migraines.

When I consulted my doctor she asked if they were preceded by vertigo.

"Yes!"

"Does your mother get migraines?"

"When she was alive, she did. Awful migraines."

"What you're having are basilar migraines. They're hereditary, usually from the mother's side, and usually preceded for ten minutes to an hour by symptoms like dizziness, nausea, slurred speech, difficulty hearing—"

"—WHAT?"

"It's not funny, Richard."

"Sorry. Okay, what do I do?"

"Get lots of sleep and exercise and try not to stress."

"Oh sure."

"Don't drink alcohol or take drugs."

"I'm in the program."

"Limit caffeine and chocolate."

"Oh God, *no coffee or chocolate?*"

"Seriously. Eat a well-balanced diet. I suggest you keep a journal of what you were doing or eating just before an attack."

"Any meds you can give me?"

"There are a few we can try you on. They're for normal migraines, but they sometimes work for basilars. If they don't work, we could try you on serotonin blockers."

"What are serotonin blockers?"

"Anti-depressants."

"Let's go straight to anti-depressants."

So now I'm on Cymbalta, which hasn't really stopped the migraines, but definitely improves my mood.

WHY I DIDN'T DATE BLACK MEN

You may have noticed that all my boyfriends were White.

Maybe it's because when I was five years old Uncle Fingers ran his hands all over me while we were supposed to be napping at Grandma Marie's.

Or maybe because when my cousins and I put on a show for the family, afterward they forced my head into a pillow and raped me.

Or maybe because a friend of my father's, a fellow comic and actor, molested me when I was twelve.

TOM

Tom and I met at Pieces, a gay bar on Christopher Street.

It was band karaoke night. A live band played the song you requested, one they knew, nothing too obscure.

But I didn't get up on stage.

Tom and I eyeballed and immediately started talking. I was a little put off at first, because right away he started using the L-word—i.e. "love." But soon, I warmed to him. He was around 50, a mix of Irish and Puerto Rican with light brown salt-and-pepper hair, brown eyes behind glasses, and a ready laugh.

He had an interesting backstory: at his wedding—yes, he was

married and lived with his wife and kids in Staten Island—he discovered that his parents were not his real parents, but his grandparents, and the woman he thought was his aunt was actually his mother.

He told me he worked for Verizon, in the company's downtown building near the Brooklyn Bridge. He was in charge of maintenance, had been at the same job for 34 years.

Ah, stability. I was ready for stability. But a wife and kids in Staten Island? Aside from being smitten with me, I couldn't figure what he wanted.

I made it clear that I was staying at a friend's studio apartment in Chelsea, a hook-up there was out of the question. He didn't press it or offer to splurge on a hotel room.

Since he worked in Manhattan though, we started hanging out in the evenings, maybe dinner, maybe a movie.

But I couldn't keep couch-surfing at my friend's studio apartment. I mentioned to Tom that I was even thinking about going back to Peoria, at which point he asked me to move in with him.

"Move in? With you and your wife and three kids?"

"Yes. I already told her. I mean, I told her I would ask you."

The next Saturday, Tom drove into the city, loaded my few belongings into his car, and we headed across the Verrazano Narrows Bridge into the wilds of Staten Island.

On the way, Tom seemed a wee bit nervous and repeated what he'd already told me about his wife, Iris, and their relationship.

Iris had a boyfriend. She spent weekends with him, leaving Tom in charge of the kids from Friday evening to Sunday afternoon.

Basically, Iris and Tom were good friends, they saw no reason to divorce or separate, particularly since they both loved the kids— Matthew, in eighth grade, and the twins, in fifth grade.

Arriving at his Staten Island neighborhood, I noticed how similar it was to my native Peoria. There were the white picket fences around nicely painted two-story houses with neatly mowed front lawns and shrubbery.

Tom's house had a little fountain on the lawn, and a porch with porch furniture—a couple of Adirondack chairs.

He introduced me to Iris. She was short, five feet or so, with dark brown hair. She greeted me warmly; we shook hands. So far, so good.

It was Tom and me upstairs, his wife and three kids downstairs.

I can tell you're thinking, *Wasn't that awkward?*

Yes. It was. At first.

As soon as I settled in, Iris took Tom across the street and pointed up at our bedroom window. She was worried that the neighbors could look in and see us.

Tom assured her that we would not make out in front of the window, we'd even keep the curtains closed.

I lived in that house with Tom, Iris, and the kids, from December 2010 until January 2018. We were family. I attended holiday parties and dinners, school events, birth and bridal showers, you name it.

I also redid the backyard, a large lot where I planted flowers and shrubs. On warm weekends we'd grill out there. Tom bought the food and I barbecued.

Eight years.

ME

I needed some alone time.

I left Staten Island and sublet an apartment in Harlem, a condo owned by my ex-wife Diane and her husband. We'd become the best of friends. She was pastor of a church in Easton, Pennsylvania, and I drove there every Sunday to attend services.

In 2015 I put together a cabaret show which I called *Love, Life, and a Few Laughs*. It debuted at the Metropolitan Room in the Flatiron District of Manhattan. I sang some songs, told a few jokes, donned outlandish wigs and costumes, and reminisced about my family.

To my surprise and delight, the show was nominated for a Manhattan Area Cabaret (MAC) Award and got me a professional manager, Bernie Furshpan.

Rain and me at the Metropolitan Room.

I was also in some films, including, to name a few: *College Debt*; *Prepper's Grove*; *Amazed by You*; *That Wasn't Supposed to Happen*; *Bachelor's Grove*.

College Debt, *with the fabulous Randy Jones of Village People.*

Looking back on my 55 years of life, I see that the main lesson I had to learn was how to love. To love others and to love myself— flaws and all. As that lesson seeped into my consciousness, a lot of the baggage I carried fell away.

Forgiveness was another biggie. Forgiving people who took advantage of me, who were mean to me, who abused me: if any of you guys are reading this, know that I forgive you. If for no other reason than for my own sake, to preserve my sanity.

Nowadays, I don't take drugs or drink alcohol. Well, except one margarita every year on my birthday.

And I'll definitely have one the day this book is published.

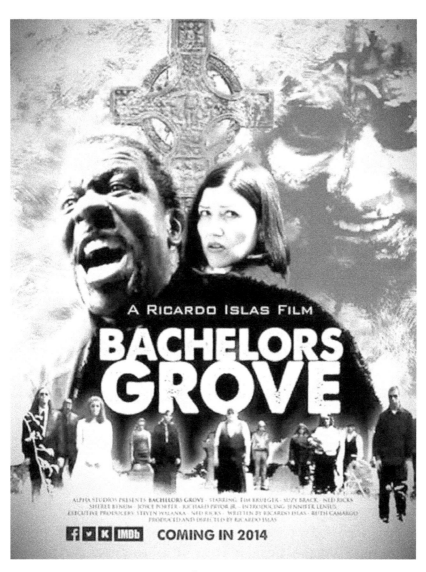

A scream.

Prepper's Grove *Obviously, I have a thing for "grove" movies.*

SISTERS

I'm in close contact with my sisters Rain, Elizabeth, Tammi, and Elanda.

Rain has a phenomenally successful career in TV, on stage, and in film. She also is the author of her own memoir about growing up with Dad: *Jokes My Father Never Taught Me.*

Rain and Dad.

She lives in Baltimore, Maryland with her daughter, Lotus, and her husband, Dave. She's artistic director of Baltimore's Strand Theater.

My sister Elanda is, like, my heart. When she was born I carried her on my hip, and when she was a little older if she got into any trouble with Mom, I'd volunteer to take the spanking for her because I didn't want her to get spanked.

Well, okay, except for that time with the screen door.

Elanda lives in Peoria, is divorced, has three boys, and works at an adult substance abuse facility, which, when you think about it, is the perfect job for a sister of mine.

Tammi also lives in Peoria. She has three adult children, two boys and a girl, and works as district manager of a cleaning company.

Tammi and Elanda in a recent shot.

Elizabeth is an associate professor at Smith College in Boston. Her specialty is history and African-American studies. She is married and has two kids, a boy and girl.

Elizabeth. "We'll always have Paris."

A FINAL THOUGHT

Whenever I meet someone for the first time and introduce myself, "Hi, Richard Pryor Jr., pleased to meet you," I sense their immediate reaction. Even if they don't express it in words, the thought is in their eyes: "Ooh, Richard Pryor's son! Tell me stuff about your dad!"

Okay, here's some stuff: Dad played a huge role in my life. He helped me out when I was in trouble, always loved me, and was there when I needed him.

But his role in my life pales in significance when measured side by side with my mother's.

A few years ago, on Mother's Day, I wrote this tribute to her and posted it on Facebook.

> My mother gave me life.
> She cared for me when I was ill.
> She took me to school and attended all my school functions and activities.
> She disciplined me—whupped my butt—often when I did not think that I deserved it. One time, she whupped me with a bag of groceries.
> I still laugh about that.
> On my wedding day, she had just been released from the hospital. Yet she would not miss the betrothal of her eldest child, not for anything.
> I was blessed with her sensitivity, compassion, and ability to give without expecting anything in return.
> As the song goes, "In my life there's been heartache and pain, I don't know if I can face it again."
> When Mom was alive, I knew I could face it again.
> Since her death, I'm not always so sure.
> Friends tell me, "It gets easier, Richard."
> I nod my head and think, no, it doesn't.
> My mom. Patricia Beatrice Price.
> Thank you for giving me life.

Thank you for making me feel special.
Thank you for allowing me to be a part of your life.
I love you and miss you.
I will never forget you.

Mom and me.

ACKNOWLEDGEMENTS

To Bernie and Joanne Furshpan, I can only say you've believed in me from day one. Thank you for welcoming me with open arms.

To Aunt Angie, I thank you for picking up when Mom left us. You have been a continuous beacon of light in my life.

To Alan and Kimberly, I thank you from the bottom of my heart. Without you this endeavor would have never been possible.

My Grey Squirrel, siblings, son, and grands, you are the reason I continue to better myself.

Thanks to the following for your contributions to this book in whatever capacity:

Thomas Allen, Frank Gordon, Elanda Steeland, Rain Pryor Vane, Barbara Mcgee, Melba LaRose, Phyllis Sharp Brecklin, Corey Dee Williams, Ann Kayman, Pastor Diane and Frederick London, Amy V. Simmons, Mark Rupp, Chris Wheeler, Bobby Anderson Jr., Lonnie Senstock, Frank Eaken, Bill Kinison, Mitzi Shore, Sharon Barnett, Ash Bennington, Eric Harrison, Kathleen Lawlor, Brian Byrd, and Mo'Nique Hicks.

Lightning Source UK Ltd.
Milton Keynes UK
UKHW020959010519
341924UK00012B/1339/P